THE
VATICAN'S
WOMEN

THE

VATICAN'S

WOMEN

FEMALE INFLUENCE AT THE HOLY SEE

PAUL HOFMANN

ST. MARTIN'S PRESS   NEW YORK

www.stmartins.com

Library of Congress Cataloging-in-Publication Data

Hofmann, Paul, 1912–
       The Vatican's women : female influence at the Holy See / Paul Hofmann.
          p.   cm.
       ISBN 0-312-27490-4
       1. Women in the Catholic Church—Vatican City—History.   2. Papacy—History.
       I. Title.

  BX2347.8.W6 H64   2002
  282'.45634'082—dc21

                                                                                        2002069827

First Edition: October 2002

10   9   8   7   6   5   4   3   2   1

To my sons, Ernesto and Alexander

CONTENTS

ACKNOWLEDGMENTS

The author wishes to express his deep gratitude to the prelates, priests, nuns, and lay employees of the Holy See who, on condition of anonymity, shared their views and experiences with him.

PREFACE

This book draws on personal observations in Rome over many years and on long talks with more than forty women serving the Vatican in various capacities: nuns and members of the laity who are or have been employees of the sprawling pontifical administration. Two female jobholders in the Vatican assisted me in my research; neither wants to be identified.

From childhood I have been familiar with the teachings, activities, special culture, and problems of the Roman Catholic Church and eventually of the Vatican. I was born into a Catholic family in Vienna, served as an altar boy at morning mass before elementary-school classes in the Votive Church near where we then were living, and later enrolled in a Catholic students' association.

In my early twenties I found myself, to my surprise, editor

in chief of the weekly newspaper of the Catholic Action movement of Vienna archdiocese, *Katholisches Leben*. When the
Nazis took over Austria in 1938, they closed the weekly,
searched our offices, and arrested our executive director, Monsignor Jakob Fried. He was sent to Dachau concentration camp.

I emigrated to Italy. Days before I left Vienna I watched
the city's archbishop, Cardinal Theodor Innitzer, stretch out
his right arm in the Nazi salute to greet the crowd that had
gathered in the Ringstrasse after he had paid a formal call on
Hitler at the Imperial Hotel. I would never forget the shameful
scene. I witnessed it and reported on it as the Vienna correspondent of the Swiss newspaper *Berner Tagblatt* of Bern, a part-
time job I had landed a couple of years earlier.

When I first arrived in Rome, I was astonished at the number of priests and nuns I saw. What are they all doing here? I
wondered. One of the sights tourists were then advised to seek
out was the Piazza Pilotta, near the Trevi Fountain, at noon-
time. From the Pontifical Gregorian University, then as now
the Catholic Church's foremost institution of higher education,
hundreds of students for the priesthood in multicolored garb
streamed out at the end of morning classes, and in ranks of
two walked into different directions for lunch at their seminaries and colleges. The Americans wore black cassocks with
blue braids and red sashes; the Scotsmen, violet cassocks with
red sashes; the members of the German-Hungarian College
were all in bright red—the Romans therefore called them the
gamberi (crayfish); and there were many other combinations of
colors. An all-male student body for a future all-male priesthood and hierarchy.

Those were the last years of Mussolini's dictatorship, and
the variety of clerical habits was matched by the regime's pot-
pourri of uniforms. There was the multiplicity of security forces
(still in existence today): the Carabinieri on foot or horseback

with red stripes on their black pants; the state police in dark blue; the Finance Guard with yellow tabs on their gray-green uniforms; the municipal cops in black or (in summer) white. There were officers and enlisted men of the army, navy, and air force, and swaggering members of the Fascist militia in black shirts and a fringed and tasseled black fez on their heads.

Walk today to the Piazza Pilotta between noon and one P.M. and you'll see swarms of young people, many in blue jeans, pouring out of the papal university; quite a few of them are female students. Some future priests will be chatting with young women also in jeans or, if they are nuns, wearing mid-calf skirts, maybe a jacket with a little cross on its lapel and a head scarf. They study theology or attend some other course on the academic menu.

Although the tempo seems glacial, women do advance a little in the church, even in Rome and even in the Vatican.

In an intellectual process that had been going on for years, I became in Rome an agnostic. Because of my newspaper work I nevertheless kept in touch with many clerics and some nuns and continued observing church affairs. To the international media, as to diplomats and governments everywhere, Rome is an important listening post, primarily because it is the seat of the papacy. Without the Vatican, the capital of Italy, a medium-sized nation, would produce mostly stories on archaeology, art, food, fashion, lifestyles, and other "soft" material for global consumption.

As a foreign correspondent for *The New York Times* on six continents during several years, I cultivated the apostolic nuncios, the pope's ambassadors, in various countries because they were usually well informed; most of them were titular archbishops, and some of them later became cardinals.

During my six years as chief of the Rome bureau of *The New York Times*, it was part of my job to follow Vatican de-

velopments closely, and I established contacts with papal officials of different levels and nationalities. The insights that I
thus gained were useful when I became chief of the United
Nations bureau of the newspaper in Manhattan. Eventually I
returned to live again in Rome.

The reader of this volume will often find only generic at-
tributions. A cult of secrecy has at all times been dominant in
the sacred palaces; nobody who lives or works in them, from
doorkeeper to cardinal, cares to become known as one who
blabs to outsiders. Nevertheless, in Rome nothing remains a
secret for long. Quite a few Vatican matters are covered by so-
called pontifical secret, meaning that anyone violating it faces
excommunication or other spiritual church punishments as
well as—what to some offenders may be far more painful—the
loss of a job.

Those Vatican secrets have nothing to do with the secret
of the confessional. Kneeling penitents reporting their sins to
the priest who is often only dimly visible behind a grate are
assured he won't disclose what he hears to any third party—
not even to the police or a magistrate if a crime has been
revealed.

Penance in early Christianity was often a public, collective
act; it still is in several Christian denominations, where it is
expressed in general terms by the congregation. The Roman
Catholic Church has stuck to the sacrament of penance as a
private one-on-one procedure detailing a person's faults. Catholic feminists suggest that women penitents should have the
option to be confessed by a female priest. The number of confessions is at any rate generally declining.

The secrets guarded at the Holy See instead are often
linked with politics, power plays, diplomatic maneuvers,
money, personality clashes, and questions of ethics anywhere
in the world or in the papal state itself.

The sources quoted in this book, even if they are nameless or have fictitious names, are all real people. I have tried to keep out what sounded like mere hearsay or scandalous tattle. Insider gossip thrives in the Vatican, as it does in all vast organizations. It always has, and through the centuries it has found its way also into the secret reports that diplomats at the pontifical court sent to their sovereigns and home governments.

Journalists and writers who specialize in Vatican affairs, known in Rome as *vaticanisti* (Vaticanologists), hear juicy and malicious rumors all the time but usually practice self-censorship in their reporting for fear of being stripped of their accreditation by the tightly run press office of the Holy See.

My personal experience is that priests of all ranks, including members of religious societies for men, gossip with more gusto than do the four hundred or so women who work in the Vatican or live there. One of the reasons is that much of the male buzz concerns advancement—which monsignor is about to become a bishop, which archbishop won't make cardinal when the pope next nominates new princes of the church, which cardinal has gone senile and lets his secretary make all decisions, and inevitably who will be the next pontiff.

Most of such gossip is strictly insiders' stuff. To outsiders, clergymen sound protective of colleagues and superiors much the way physicians tend to be whenever criticism is leveled at one of their profession.

Careerism burgeons in the Vatican. Women are useful to the papacy in many ways but until now have had no chance for rising in its service beyond a modest level. The Vatican glass ceiling is even lower than it is in the most patriarchal business corporation, and the metaphorical glass is tinted with prelatical purple and is plainly visible.

I

THE POPESS COMPLEX

Through the centuries Roman gossip and folklore bestowed the nickname "popess" on various women who were believed to wield undue power or influence at the summit of the church. The prototype of them all—whether a myth or (less likely) a historical figure—was supposed to have actually been pontiff herself for some time and to have performed credibly in the job until she was unmasked by biology.

The story of "Popess Joan" was generally accepted as true until the end of the Middle Ages. The *New Catholic Encyclopedia** recalls that Jan Hus, the Bohemian religious reformer, reproached the assembled prelates and theologians at the Council of Constance (1414–18) "with Popess Joan whose existence no one denied." Bringing up the unwelcome old tale

---

*Prepared by the editorial staff at the Catholic University of America (New York: McGraw-Hill, 1967).

didn't do any good to Hus; the council condemned him as a heretic for doctrinal reasons (not for the Popess Joan story) and had him burned at the stake in 1415.

The saga of Popess Joan (in Latin: Papissa Iohanna) comes in different versions, narrated by chroniclers and preachers of the thirteenth and fourteenth centuries. They all apparently drew their material from an old Roman popular and clerical tradition, which may have had its origins in the notorious role that the influential and manipulative women of the Theophylactus clan (see below) played in the early tenth century.

The written sources, including reports by Dominican and Franciscan authors, have as their subject a woman, either German or English, usurping the papal throne for a brief period in the ninth, tenth, or eleventh century. The female impostor's real name is variously supposed to have been Agnes, Gilberta, Glaucia, or—in German—Jutta.

The most widely accepted account was that of the Polish Dominican friar Martin of Troppau (now Opava in the Czech Republic, near the Polish border). According to Friar Martin, Pope Leo IV (847–55), a Roman, was succeeded by one Iohannes Angelicus ("English John" or "Angelic John"?) who styled herself John VIII; nobody suspected that the new head of the church was a woman.

A native of Mainz in Germany, she completed her studies in Athens, Friar Martin reports. When she was to return home, disguised as a man, she stopped in Rome. In the papal city she impressed everybody with her learning, was prevailed upon to stay, and became an ecclesiastical notary. She soon was made a cardinal and, after Leo IV's death, was elected pope.

She exercised the pontifical office with competence and dignity until her true sex was discovered. Secretly she had taken a lover and had become pregnant, concealing her condition under her heavy liturgical vestments. During a papal procession on the road leading from the Colosseum to the Basilica of St. John Lateran, the historic see of the bishops of Rome, labor pains set in and she gave birth, prematurely it seems, to a male infant near the Church of St. Clement.

This church was erected in the fourth century and dedicated to the third successor of the Apostle Saint Peter; it was rebuilt in the early twelfth century, still exists today, and is the best-preserved medieval basilica in Rome. That Popess Joan's deception was clamorously uncovered near that church, now known as San Clemente, is unanimously affirmed by Martin of Troppau and the other chroniclers, although they disagree on many other details.

The impostor's punishment is variously described. The consensus is that she and her child died or were put to death. Popular speculation inevitably surrounded the case with lurid fantasies, alleging among many other things that the father of the popess's baby was Satan.

According to the Vatican's official chronology of the pontiffs, Saint Leo IV was succeeded in 855 by Benedict III, a Roman who reigned for less than three years, and was followed by Saint Nicholas the Great, another Roman (858–67). An antipope, Anastasius, known as the Librarian, is listed between brackets as having claimed the papal throne for just a few days in 855 and having died in 880. A Pope John VIII (872–882) is well documented because he prevented the Saracens who had invaded southern Italy from entering Rome by promising them an annual tribute; he was also deeply involved in the politics and wars of Charlemagne's successors and of various nobles in Italy. For the Vatican today, a female John VIII never existed.

In the minds of the Romans, however, the story of Popess Joan was reinforced by the discovery during the Renaissance of an ancient statue representing a male or female god or

priest—accounts differ—with a serving boy. It was dug up near
the traditional route of papal processions. On a stone nearby
was a Latin inscription that was interpreted in different ways.
Both finds were on display for some time near the Church of
San Clemente, but Pope Saint Pius V (1566–72) is said to have
ordered the removal of both the statue and the inscription;
there is no trace of either anywhere today. A sculpture, believed to represent Popess Joan, was placed, together with statues of other popes, in the Cathedral of Siena, Tuscany, about
the year 1500, but it too has disappeared.

Popess Joan's supposed moment of truth near the Church
of San Clemente is believed to have prompted medieval popes
to change the route of their traditional procession from what
is today Via di San Giovanni in Laterano to the parallel street,
Via dei Santi Quattro, to avoid passing the spot. Whenever
the pope today visits the Lateran, he arrives there either by
helicopter or by car with an escort of security officers on motorcycles, taking various routes, depending on the traffic situation. No formal papal cortege takes place in the area anymore.
The Church of San Clemente has long been in the charge of
Irish Dominicans.

An early literary adaptation of the Popess Joan tale can be
found in *De Claris Mulieribus* (Concerning Famous Women),
which Giovanni Boccaccio wrote in Latin between 1355 and
1359.* The book by the French-born, Florentine-educated poet
and novelist is probably the first collection of women's biog-
raphies in world literature. Its tone is much more sober than
his famous *Decameron*, written twenty years earlier in sparkling
and often mocking Tuscan idiom.

De Claris Mulieribus is evidence of the interest in women

---

*Published in the original text with English translation and annotations by
Guido A. Guarino (New Brunswick, N.J.: Rutgers University Press, 1963).

and sympathy for them that mark Boccaccio's entire oeuvre. Popess Joan is no. 99 in a gallery of 104 portraits of female protagonists, starting with Eve. Many of them are mythical, like Semiramis, Juno, or Helen of Troy; others are historical, like Julia, the daughter of Julius Caesar, and Ioanna, queen of Sicily, Naples, and Jerusalem (no. 104). Boccaccio did not include early Christian martyrs or medieval saints in his series of notable women.

The Joan who was to occupy the papal throne is characterized as "a woman whose unheard-of audacity made her known to the whole world and posterity." Boccaccio gives credit to the theory that she was a native of Mainz on the Rhine and that her original name was Gilberta. Still young, she had an affair with a student and "cast away maidenly fear and shame and fled from her father's house" to study, dressed as a man, with her lover in England. There everyone took her for a brilliant young cleric. When her lover died, she went to Rome, "already mature in years" (which in Boccaccio's time may have meant in her early thirties), and lectured there for a number of years.

Boccaccio places the start of Joan's pontifical adventure in the period after the death of Pope Leo V in 903, although most sources date it at 855, following Saint Leo IV's death. The cardinals, the writer reports, unanimously elected her to the papacy with the name of John VIII. "A woman, then, was the Vicar of Christ on earth. God, from on high, was merciful to his people and did not allow a woman to hold so lofty a place, govern so many peoples, and deceive them with such a wicked fraud."

Many readers of Boccaccio in his own day would have sensed authorial irony in these lines. He stresses that Joan until then had been "remarkably virtuous" but having arrived at the pinnacle of the church, "fell prey to the ardor of lust." She found "someone who would secretly mount St. Peter's successor and assuage her lecherous itching." She became pregnant and publicly gave birth between the Colosseum and the Church of St. Clement "without the presence of a midwife."

The cardinals threw the "wretched woman" into a dungeon, where she died. No mention of her child. Boccaccio notes that "down to our times" [the mid-fourteenth century] the popes during their traditional processions from the Colosseum to the Lateran at the halfway point turn away to take an alternate route because of their hatred of the place."

The story of Popess Joan, endorsed by a writer of Boccaccio's stature, became a favorite theme of the pamphleteers of the Protestant Reformation. The Jesuit scholar and cardinal Saint Robert Bellarmine (1542–1621) and other Roman Catholic apologists confuted it as a fable. They received authoritative support from the French Protestant minister and historian David Blondel (1591–1655), who in two treatises, displaying his profound scholarship, declared the tradition of a woman on the papal throne to be a myth. Almost all reputable modern historians likewise reject the Popess Joan story.

A raunchy byproduct is the Roman folk tale of a secret rite performed after each papal election: before proclaiming the new head of the church, the cardinals have him sit on a chair with an opening in the seat and a young cleric crouches underneath to make sure by hand that the newly chosen personage possesses male genitals. Some collectors of historical anecdotes assert that the bodily examination was performed until the end of the sixteenth century or even later. Today quite a few Romans earnestly insist that the test of papal manhood is still a part of secret conclave procedures. This hardy perennial of local folklore may have originated from popular reinterpretation of the function of perforated marble or porphyry chairs *(sellae pertuseae)* dug up in the ruins of ancient *thermae,* or public baths, during excavations in the Renaissance era.

How deeply the story or legend of Popess Joan is rooted in popular culture in Italy, France, and other Roman Catholic countries may be seen from her appearance in card games. Popess, complete with triple crown on her head and baby in her arms, is included in old decks of cards along with such characters as Hermit and Justice.

Scheming Females

Undoubtedly historical, on the other hand, were Theodora and Marozia, whose memory may have given rise to the popess story. Edward Gibbon in his *Decline and Fall of the Roman Empire* calls them "two sister prostitutes" whose wealth, beauty, and scheming produced their enormous influence on ecclesiastical politics in the early tenth century. "The most strenuous of their lovers," Gibbon indignantly proceeds, "were rewarded with the Roman miter. . . . The bastard son, the grandson and the great-grandson of Marozia, a rare genealogy, were seated in the chair of St. Peter."

The English historian—who early in life had converted to Roman Catholicism, only to return soon to the Protestant faith—was never indulgent of the Church of Rome (or Christianity in general), yet he discounted "the fable of a female pope."

Marozia and Theodora domineered in Rome in a turbulent epoch, the nadir of the papacy. The city was haphazardly run by a clique of nobles to which the sisters' family belonged. The lords of Tusculum, ensconced in their fortress in the hillside twenty-five miles southeast of Rome, as well as the Frankish marquesses of Tuscany to the north and the German emperors of the Saxon dynasty, who with their troops periodically invaded Italy, continually interfered in the affairs of church government. Popes were created, controlled, humiliated, insulted, mistreated, deposed, imprisoned, and murdered at the whims of powerful outsiders.

One of the pontiffs of that dark era, Sergius III (904–11), had as his mistress Marozia, a daughter of Theophylactus, a papal dignitary, and of Theodora the Elder who claimed the title of *senatrix* (woman senator). The pope's licentious affair is reported by the *Liber Pontificalis* (Pontifical Book), a collection of medieval chronicles and biographical information concerning early popes that is an important source of church history, repeatedly quoted by the official Vatican yearbook (*Annuario Pontificio*) of our age.

In 931 Marozia had one of her sons, supposedly by Pope Sergius III, elected pontiff with the name of John XI. He nominally reigned for five years, a virtual prisoner in the Vatican, while his mother was in effect wielding pontifical powers for some time—a "popess" in all but name.

Marozia was thrice married: to Alberic I, duke of Spoleto, in 905; to Guido, marquess of Tuscany, in 925; and to Hugh, a Burgundian who styled himself "king of Italy," in 932. The elevation of her and (presumably) Pope Sergius III's son to the papacy as John XI signaled the peak of her power.

Her downfall came quickly. Another son (by her first husband), Alberic II, fomented an uprising of the Roman nobility and had her captured. Marozia was imprisoned in the Castel Sant'Angelo near the Vatican, and nothing was heard of her after the rebellion. She may have died of natural causes or violently in the papal fortress.

Marozia's son Alberic II governed Rome and the church sternly, though not as a pope, and on his deathbed in 954 had the cowed nobles and prelates swear to make his son Octavian the next pope as soon as the pontifical throne was vacant. After the death of the powerless Pope Agapitus II in 955, Octavian was indeed elected pontiff, assuming the name John XII; he was not yet twenty years old.

A respected Lombard chronicler, Liutprand, reports that Marozia's grandson John XII turned the Lateran Palace—then the papal residence—into a "school of prostitution" and that his outrageous conduct prevented female would-be pilgrims from visiting the tombs of the Apostles Peter and Paul, meaning Rome, for fear of rape.

It took more than another hundred years filled with scandal, violence, confusion, and schisms—with nearly thirty popes and antipopes—before the forceful Benedictine monk Hildebrand of Tuscany, as Pope Gregory VII, managed to reform the church. Among other things, he enforced the rule of celibacy for all clerics under his obedience. He humbled the German emperor Henry IV at Canossa in 1077, only to be driven by him into exile a few years later. Rome proclaimed Gregory VII a saint in 1728.

When he was at the height of his political power at the Castle of Canossa, north of Bologna, in 1077, Gregory VII was the guest of Matilda, duchess or margravine of Tuscia (Tuscany). During three decades the well-educated, rich, and influential Matilda, known in her time as the "great countess," lent her support to four consecutive pontiffs against the German (Holy Roman) emperors. In a rare gesture of Vatican gratitude for a woman, Pope Urban VIII, a Florentine, had her remains transferred to Rome and reburied in St. Peter's in 1635.

The "great countess" bequeathed her vast estates to the church, but the papacy was able to take possession of only some of them, while others were won by different claimants.

Catherine's Letters

Another exceptional woman, the visionary and mystic Saint
Catherine of Siena (1347–80), could offer the head of the
church only advice and prayers, yet her impact on the papacy
was of historic importance. Only twenty-nine years old but already considered a living saint, she went to Avignon, France,
to urge Pope Gregory XI to end the nearly seventy-year "Bab-
ylonian captivity" of the pontiffs and take the government of
the church back to Rome. Astonishingly, the illiterate quasi-
nun in the long black cape of a penitent persuaded Gregory,
an erudite Frenchman, to take just that momentous step,
against the opposition of his cardinals and court and despite
great odds.

Caterina Benincasa, the twenty-fourth of twenty-five children of a moderately well-to-do dyer with a large house on the
outskirts of Siena, never went to school. As a late-born girl,
she never received any formal education and could speak only
her soft Sienese dialect. Yet most of the nearly four hundred
letters that she dictated to disciples were addressed to popes,
the emperor, military leaders, and other important personages
and were taken seriously by them. (She wrote also to a prostitute in Perugia and to the prison inmates of Siena.) Her prose
in the vernacular of Tuscany—used also by Dante in the *Divine
Comedy*—has enriched the Italian language and literature.

At the age of six Saint Catherine experienced her first sei-
zure, or vision. Soon she began observing a regimen of fasting
and self-mortification, committing herself to lifelong poverty,
chastity, and obedience. At fifteen she was admitted into the
Third Order of the Dominicans. As a mere tertiary (a layperson
associated with a religious order), she never took formal vows.
She restricted herself to a narrow room, her "cell," in her father's house. Near the end of her life one of her followers gave

her a former fortress of the republic of Siena on the Belcaro Hill, three miles northwest of the city walls, and she had it transformed into a convent with a chapel.

By her early twenties Saint Catherine must have possessed remarkable charisma; she was credited with miraculous powers and gathered a group of devotees around herself. She also became a kind of one-woman lobby for the papacy and for peace in a tempestuous epoch. The main instrument of her pressure tactics were those famed letters, of which 370 have been conserved (she probably wrote more, which have been lost). Some were translated into Latin, then the language of educated people all over Europe.

Saint Catherine repeatedly insisted that it wasn't she who admonished the recipients of her letters but God, who spoke through her. The style is muscular, even authoritarian. The word *virile* recurs; letter 233 exhorts Pope Gregory XI to act "virilely." Catherine's metaphors are homespun: "Let's not sleep in the bed of negligence," "the demons flee from divine charity the way the housefly escapes . . ."

The Siena dyer's daughter traveled to Avignon in 1376 as an ambassador from the republic of Florence, which then was in conflict with the pope and had been struck by him with the interdict, the suspension of sacraments and other spiritual benefits. Gregory XI in a formal audience addressed the young woman in Latin; she fearlessly answered in the Sienese dialect, which was rendered into Latin by her father confessor, closest friend, and future biographer, Raimondo of Capua, a Dominican.

Saint Catherine stayed in Avignon the entire summer of 1376, continually entreating the pope by speech and letter to move the Holy See permanently back to Rome. The proposed move caused outrage in the papal court, particularly among the "ladies of Avignon," the influential female relatives and mistresses of cardinals and other prelates; they detested the thought of abandoning the good life in the French city and its rambling papal palace.

Gregory XI, however, did make the epochal decision. He left his palace on horseback on September 13, 1376, despite the tears and cries of his own mother, and in Marseilles he embarked on a sea voyage that at one point threatened to end in shipwreck. Catherine followed the pontiff in part on land, in part by sea, and met him again in Genoa before returning to Siena.

At the end of a rough voyage with various stopovers, Pope Gregory XI arrived in Rome on January 13, 1377. Riding a white mule like Jesus in Jerusalem, the French pontiff was cheered by the Roman populace and took up residence in the Vatican. The Eternal City was then a scruffy place of at most thirty thousand souls, full of the abandoned ruins of past grandeur, with foxes and even wolves roaming in the underbrush.

Soon after his arrival Gregory XI sent Saint Catherine, who had remained in Siena, to Florence on a peace mission. There, she lived through local riots and once had to hide in a garden to escape a murderous mob, but she eventually brought about an accord between the Florentines and the Holy See.

Pope Gregory XI had meanwhile died and an Italian, Urban VI, was elected as his successor. The French cardinals who had reluctantly followed Gregory XI to Rome declared Urban VI's election null and void and chose an antipope, Robert of Geneva, who styled himself Clement VII and moved back to Avignon. The Great Schism was on, and would last until the Council of Constance (1414–18), when the split in the Western church would be ended by the election of Pope Martin V, a Roman.

The pontiff in the Vatican, Urban VI, in the face of the ecclesiastical rebellion, called Saint Catherine to Rome and asked her to address the cardinals who had remained loyal to him. She came and resolutely backed Urban VI against his rival in Avignon.

Catherine stayed in Rome, living in a house near the Pantheon with her mother and two dozen male and female disciples. Every day she walked to St. Peter's on the opposite side of the Tiber and spent hours in prayer there. Weakened by arthritis and undernourishment brought on by unceasing fasting, she died on April 29, 1380.

Saint Catherine was canonized by Pope Pius II, a native of a town near Siena, in 1461. Her remains rest in the main altar of the Church of Santa Maria sopra Minerva, near the Pantheon in Rome, which is in charge of the Dominican order. The saint's head, enclosed in a reliquary, was transferred to Siena and is revered there in a chapel of the Church of San Domenico, a shrine of the Dominicans.

Pope Pius XII in 1939, shortly before the outbreak of World War II, proclaimed Saint Catherine of Siena the heavenly co-patron of Italy, together with Saint Francis of Assisi. Pope Paul VI in 1970 solemnly pronounced the illiterate dyer's daughter to be a Doctor of the Church, a posthumous rank she shares with such eminent philosophers and theologians as Saint Thomas Aquinas.

Acting Pope Lucrezia

Fast-forward to the beginning of the sixteenth century. In that turbulent—though culturally immensely productive—epoch the papacy was deeply embroiled in Italian and European power politics. Rome had become a byword for nepotism, greed, corruption, and immorality.

Pope Alexander VI, the former Rodrigo Borja (italianized

into *Borgia*), was ruling the church in the style of a secular Renaissance prince. He astutely maneuvered among the major Italian powers—the duchy of Milan, the republic of Venice, and the Spanish-governed kingdom of Naples—as well as among the smaller states and lordships. King Charles VIII of France had just invaded the Italian peninsula with thirty thousand soldiers and marched almost unopposed across Tuscany and the papal territories, as far south as Naples. On his way back with an army that the "Neapolitan disease" (syphilis) and other mishaps had reduced to ten thousand men, Charles VIII was still strong enough to inflict a humbling defeat at Fornovo, near Bologna, in 1495 on the numerous troops of an Italian "Holy League" alliance backed by Pope Alexander VI. The commanding general of the Italian coalition, Duke Francesco Gonzaga of Mantua, all the same claimed that he had actually won at Fornovo, but Europe wasn't duped, and King Charles VIII with the remainder of his army reached France as a victor in the Italian wars.

In the late summer of 1501 Alexander VI left Rome in high spirits to inspect the towns and fortresses south and east of the city that his son, Cesare Borgia, with his mercenaries had just wrested from Roman nobles. The conquests were to be incorporated into the papal state.

For the duration of his absence from Rome the Spanish pontiff left his daughter Lucrezia Borgia in charge of the Vatican. She was given full authority to run the papal administration, to open all letters addressed to the head of the church, except those dealing with strictly ecclesiastical matters (how could she know their contents unless she broke the seals?), and to take appropriate action.

Thus, at the age of twenty-one, Lucrezia for a few weeks was in effect a deputy pontiff. The old sobriquet *popess* was again heard in Rome. Some people in the Vatican, both in the city and abroad, were shocked, but many Romans didn't consider it very odd that the head of the church—in open violation of the law of priestly celibacy—had children by his mistresses and employed them in ecclesiastical governance. In Renaissance Rome, children of popes, cardinals, and lesser prelates (sometimes declared to be their "nephews" and "nieces") abounded and enjoyed various privileges. Rather, the scandalous reputation that Lucrezia had already acquired caused some outrage.

Lucrezia was beautiful: slim, of medium height, with long blond hair and gray-blue eyes. Pinturicchio, Alexander VI's favorite painter, is believed to have used the pope's adolescent daughter as his model for Saint Catherine of Alexandria in one of the frescoes of his *Lives of the Saints* cycle (1492–95) in a room of the Vatican's Borgia Apartment. This presumed likeness and the few other, less controversial portraits of an older Lucrezia that have survived show her with an oval face, a slightly receding chin, and full lips.

When Lucrezia became virtually an acting pope, she already had an equivocal history—since late infancy she had been a passive or willing tool in the political machinations of her father and her brother Cesare.

She was one of the children whom the future pope, then an influential cardinal, had by an attractive Roman woman of northern Italian descent, Vannozza Cattanei (or de Cataneis in the latinizing fashion of the epoch), the daughter of a humble painter. Lucrezia received a good education under the tutelage of a niece of her father (this one a real niece, not a clandestine daughter). Contemporary sources describe Alexander and Vannozza's girl as bright and fun-loving; she liked to dance and spoke good Latin in addition to Spanish, Italian, and French. Among themselves the Borgias conversed in the dialect of Alexander's native Valencia region. Lucrezia was said to have been able to read a little Greek, which at the time was as exceptional as it would be for a society woman today.

At eleven years of age—not too early, according to the standards of noble families in that era—Lucrezia was already in the marriage market. Her father first promoted two consecutive engagements, each broken off when a seemingly more promising candidate turned up. Eventually she wed Count Giovanni Sforza, lord of Pesaro and a relative of the powerful duke of Milan. At thirteen, Lucrezia was countess of Pesaro, and briefly she lived with her husband in that fishing port on the Adriatic Sea but was evidently bored there and soon returned to Rome.

Three years later Alexander VI and his son Cesare—who at eighteen had become a cardinal—decided that Lucrezia's husband had lost his political-military usefulness. A Vatican commission dissolved the marriage on the ground of nonconsummation. The count of Pesaro was thus given what amounted to a church certificate of impotence; he angrily reacted by spreading charges of incest in the Borgia family.

Libelists gleefully took up the allegation and scoffed in Latin verses that Lucrezia had been bedded by her father, her brother, or both. The lubricious accusations, which were never proved, stuck to Lucrezia and the Borgia court through the centuries.

Much more likely were insistent rumors that while waiting for her marriage annulment in Rome, Lucrezia had had an affair with a young Spanish chamberlain in her father's retinue, Pedro Calderón (whom everybody called Perotto). She may even have secretly given birth to a child by him in 1498. The fact is that the bodies of Calderón and of one of Lucrezia's personal maids, Pentesilea (who may have had a part in the amorous intrigue), were fished out of the Tiber. There is no record of Lucrezia's baby, if there was one.

The river flowing past the papal fortress of Castel Sant'-Angelo, close to the Vatican, yielded any number of corpses during those somber years. In 1497 the body of Lucrezia's older brother Juan had been spotted in the Tiber; whispers all over Rome were that Cesare had commissioned the murder of his brother, a general, to get rid of a rival standing in the way of his limitless ambition. The following year Cesare Borgia shed his cardinal's purple to become an unencumbered player in Italian power politics.

Alexander VI and Cesare now proceeded to the task of selecting one among several eager candidates for the hand of the pope's daughter. They picked a bastard member of the royal family of Naples, Alfonso of Aragon, duke of Bisceglie in Italy's Apulia region. The idea was to establish a new tie between the Vatican and the kingdom of Naples, theoretically a fiefdom of the papacy.

Lucrezia continued living in the Vatican or in a nearby building, usually in the company of her second husband; she appeared to like him better than she did the first. Between parties and dances at the papal court, Lucrezia bore Alfonso a son, Rodrigo, who for most of his short life would live in southern Italy.

Political alignments in those years were as unstable as mercury, and the Borgias found it advisable to seek a rapprochement with France, which was about to conquer the duchy of Milan. Eventually Alfonso, too, became an embarrassment because his family were enemies of the French. For some time Lucrezia's husband was sent back to Naples while Alexander asked her to serve as papal governor of Spoleto in Umbria, a church possession; she resided there in the huge fortress glowering on the city from a hilltop.

In July 1500 Lucrezia's second husband, who had drifted back to Rome, was ambushed by unidentified thugs on the steps of St. Peter's at night and was grievously wounded. Bleeding, he was carried into the Apostolic Palace. Under the care of Lucrezia and his own sister, Sancha of Aragon, he slowly seemed to recover, but less than five weeks after the first aggression, a detachment of Cesare Borgia's troops burst into the papal apartment in the Vatican's Borgia Tower, arrested Alfonso's doctors, and strangled Lucrezia's husband in his sickroom.

Lucrezia took her husband's murder badly, which appears to have surprised her father and brother. The twenty-year-old widow's screams filled the papal apartment, and she wept openly in the pope's presence, much to his annoyance. There was also open estrangement between Lucrezia and her brother Cesare, who until then had always been very close. Eventually she retired to a papal fortress in the ancient town of Nepi, north of Rome, to the pope's relief, it may be assumed.

While Cesare Borgia with the support of French forces attempted to carve out a state of his own in the Romagna in the northeastern corner of central Italy, special envoys from various parts of Italy and from France arrived at the papal court—some just a few weeks after the assassination of Lucrezia's second husband—to ask for her hand on behalf of divers noblemen. Borgia power was then peaking, and association with the papal family seemed highly desirable to many ambitious and influential people. Alexander VI pondered how his recently bereaved daughter could be advantageously remarried.

Lucrezia was back in Rome after a few months of mourning and solitude in Nepi, and was told of the negotiations for a third marriage. The Venetian ambassador reported home that once, when Alexander VI in front of courtiers admonished her in a fatherly tone to think of her future and mentioned one of her suitors, a southern Italian duke, Lucrezia's face hardened and she declined to discuss any matrimonial projects because "my husbands end up evilly."

In the beginning of 1501 Lucrezia's mood appeared to have softened. Diplomatic contacts between the Vatican and Duke Ercole Id'Este of Ferrara were envisaging a marriage between his eldest son, Alfonso, and the pope's daughter. It looked like a brilliant match for the young widow: the Estes were one of Italy's oldest aristocratic families, and their duchy, Ferrara, was a solid little state, theoretically a papal vicariate but in reality sovereign.

Alexander VI and Cesare Borgia favored the marital project because it would further the family's territorial aspirations. Lucrezia herself began to consider Alfonso d'Este as a possible third husband, and secret talks between the Vatican and Ferrara regarding such weighty matters as the young widow's dowry started.

It was in part to emphasize Lucrezia's political importance in the eyes of the no-nonsense Ferrarese, and thus enhance her value in the bargaining process, that Alexander VI later in 1501 appointed her as his lieutenant with full powers to run the Vatican while he was absent from Rome. The pope recommended that whenever his daughter needed advice, she should turn to the dean of the Sacred College, Cardinal Jorge Costa, a Portuguese.

Maria Bellonci in her well-researched biography of Lucrezia* relates that one day when the pope's young daughter and the aged cardinal were working together on a document, she assured Costa that she knew how to write. The Portuguese, as if to put her in her place as a mere woman, facetiously asked, "*Ubi est penna vostra?*" (Where is your pen?) and both broke into laughter, which echoed through the Apostolic Palace. (The double entendre sounds more ribald in spoken Latin than in English because of the assonance of *penna* and *penis*.)

---

*Maria Bellonci, *Lucrezia Borgia* (Milan: Mondadori, 1959), p. 218.

On the whole, Lucrezia appears to have done a competent job as vice pope. Her father returned to Rome; the marriage pacts with the house of Este were perfected, signed, and sealed; and the Vatican became the setting for lavish festivities to celebrate Cesare Borgia's recent military successes and augur well for Lucrezia's matrimonial-dynastic fortunes.

Scandals and a Wedding

Two shocking episodes stand out, both involving Lucrezia as well as Cesare and the pope. Both are attested by Johannes Burchard, or Burkhard (italianized in Rome as Burcardo), from Strasbourg. The staid, well-off Alsatian had, as was usual in the Renaissance era, bought the office of master of ceremonies at the papal court; four hundred gold ducats had been the price. Burchard kept a diary, which survives, recording in detail what he did and saw in papal service, most of the time without commenting or expressing outrage. Several of his reports have been corroborated by other sources. Historians tend to believe that Burchard was accurate in his observations, although pro-Borgia apologists allege that he was secretly hostile to Alexander VI and his relatives, and invented things that never happened.

Burchard's diary and, independently, a Florentine at the Vatican recorded that on Sunday, October 31, 1501, Pope Alexander VI, Cesare Borgia, and Lucrezia with their intimates dined in the Apostolic Palace. At the end of the banquet the doors were thrown open and fifty Roman courtesans, apparently rounded up in the streets by Cesare's soldiers, were brought into the hall. They were asked to dance, first clothed and then naked, with the men present. As the night proceeded, the prostitutes, now on all fours, had to compete for candied chestnuts that the revelers threw to the floor. The bacchanal ended with a contest among the men for the captive women, who seem to have been rewarded with money and other gifts before being dismissed.

Eleven days later, if Burchard is to be believed, papal servants near the Vatican spotted a team of mares carrying loads of timber. The animals were freed from their burdens and taken into a courtyard of the Apostolic Palace. Four stallions from the papal stables were released into the courtyard, where they fought over the mares. Alexander VI and Lucrezia watched the bestial scene from a window and laughed heartily.

The period of Vatican gaiety before Lucrezia's third wedding also featured more refined entertainments—classical plays, including Plauto's *Maenechmi* (which bored Alexander VI), concerts, and dances. Lucrezia's solemn proxy wedding to Alfonso d'Este, who had not moved from Ferrara, on December 30, 1501, was surrounded by pageants and merrymaking all over Rome. Three days later Cesare Borgia starred in a bullfight in St. Peter's Square in a gold-embroidered costume, first on horseback as toreador, then on foot as matador.

The square in front of the then badly dilapidated old Basilica of St. Peter must be imagined without the colonnades that Bernini would build sixty years later. Work on the grandiose new Church of St. Peter was to start in earnest only under Pope Julius II (1503–13), Michelangelo's patron. The Borgia apartment, brilliantly frescoed by Pinturicchio, is today a part of the sight-seeing circuit of the Vatican Museums. It now looks rather dark, but it was bright at the time of the Borgias because the buildings in front of it had not yet gone up. Julius II refused to use the rooms where "the accursed Borgias" had dwelled, and established his living quarters on the floor above them.

On January 6, 1502, Lucrezia at last set out for Ferrara. Her retinue was made up of nearly a thousand persons—Roman and

Ferrarese nobles, high prelates, Vatican lay officials, maids of honor, personal assistants, court jesters, servants, and a strong contingent of soldiers. A troop of pack mules carried chests with Lucrezia's dowry of seventy thousand gold ducats, which the papal treasury had somehow managed to scrape together, and the bride's rich personal jewelry.

The 275-mile journey by way of Spoleto, Urbino, Rimini, and Bologna, interrupted by several stops to allow local authorities to pay homage to the pontiff's daughter, took more than three weeks. Lucrezia saw her new husband for the first time on the outskirts of Bologna, where he had ridden out to meet her without the restraints of ceremonial. In Ferrara the celebrations in which the entire city took part lasted a week. Duke Ercole I's court cooks came up with a new pasta variety in honor of Lucrezia: golden ribbons of dough meant to allude to her blond hair. Thus fettuccine was invented to become one of the glories of the rich Emilia-Romagna cuisine.

Lucrezia's life in Ferrara is outside the scope of this book. She frequently corresponded with her father but would never see him again, and received several visits by her brother Cesare. Yet she gradually slipped out of the Borgia thrall, surviving the quick collapse of Borgia power after Pope Alexander VI's unexpected death in 1503, soon followed by Cesare Borgia's departure on a safe-conduct for Spain.

In 1505 Duke Ercole I d'Este died, and Lucrezia, as wife of his eldest son, Alfonso, became duchess of Ferrara. In 1508 she bore her husband an heir (who would become Duke Ercole II), and later three other children. Always vying with her sister-in-law and perpetual rival, the brilliant Isabella d'Este, in displays of fashion and intellectual endeavors, Lucrezia gathered a coterie of poets (like Ariosto), artists (like Titian), and humanists around her. She received adulatory letters from such great Renaissance figures as Pietro Bembo, who was later to become a cardinal, and carried on a well-documented affair—mostly in writing—with Duke Francesco Gonzaga, Isabella's husband and the self-proclaimed victor in the Battle of Fornovo.

Lucrezia's own husband, Duke Alfonso, was often absent from Ferrara to inspect gun foundries and fortresses, his consuming interest, and she increasingly occupied herself with Ferrarese public affairs. She looked after the dukedom's nunneries and monasteries, founded a convent, and through personal help in needy cases earned a measure of affection among the population. Lucrezia died in 1519.

Vatican Queen

Baroque Rome, as always brimming with gossip, was first thrilled, then amused, soon scandalized, and eventually bored by a royal eccentric from the north. As an exile in Rome, the former Queen Christina of Sweden (1626–89) was the guest of five consecutive popes and a fixture of the pontifical court. Her sensational abdication from the throne and her conversion from Lutheranism—the state church in her country—to the Roman Catholic faith in 1654 was hailed by champions of the Counter-Reformation as a triumph of the papacy.

Ex-Queen Christina wasn't the first highborn Swedish woman who for religious reasons relocated to Rome. Three centuries earlier Saint Birgitta (or Bridget) of Sweden had moved there to be near the tombs of the Apostles Peter and Paul. Birgitta, then about fifty years old, was the widow of a Swedish nobleman and mother of eight children (including Saint Catherine of Sweden, an abbess). Her husband, Ulf Gudmarrson, had died during a pilgrimage with her to the famous Spanish shrine of St. James of Compostela.

Saint Birgitta was a contemporary of Saint Catherine of Siena, but the two apparently never met. She reached literary fame in the late Middle Ages through her mystical *Revelations*, which was edited and translated into Latin by churchmen and was widely read all over Europe. She founded an order of nuns later known as the Brigittines, and sought to obtain papal recognition for it through the ecclesiastical bureaucracy in Rome, which was in permanent contact with Avignon, but it would take her twenty years to receive approval from Pope Urban V. Her charitable work made her very popular in Rome, where she died in 1373. Pope Boniface IX canonized her in 1391.

The Church of Santa Brigida (Italian for Saint Birgitta) in the Piazza Farnese marks the house where the saint lived. But with all her holiness, piety, and good works, she never made a splash in Roman life as did ex-Queen Christina.

Sweden in the seventeenth century was a major European power, which under King Gustavus II Adolphus had decisively intervened in the Thirty Years' War, deeply penetrating with its armies into the European continent. Gustavus Adolphus's daughter, Christina, was only six years old when she succeeded to the throne upon his death in the Battle of Lützen, Prussia (which the Swedes won), against the Catholic imperial forces in 1632.

Until her eighteenth year Christina was under the tutelage of her father's chancellor, Count Axel Oxenstierna, and received a careful academic and diplomatic education while the able and loyal Oxenstierna was running the country very much like a king. She was a good student. When she assumed full royal powers, she became to her subjects the "king" of Sweden, not the queen; as in Hungary, the male style was used even when the ruler was a woman, which was just fine with her.

Of rather short stature, Christina was convinced (probably with reason) that she was unattractive; she dressed carelessly

and liked to wear heavy men's shoes or boots, yet from childhood always conducted herself with remarkable dignity. Something of an intellectual, she called the French philosopher and
mathematician René Descartes to her splendid court (he
caught a cold and died soon after arriving in Stockholm in
1650) and also patronized other foreign scholars, such as the
Dutch jurist Hugo Grotius. During her ten-year reign she be-
haved erratically, inexpertly and unsuccessfully dabbling in diplomatic negotiations to end the Thirty Years' War; showed no
gratitude at all to her former mentor, Oxenstierna; and displayed a preference for distinguished foreigners such as the
Spanish ambassador. She stubbornly resisted entreaties from the
dignitaries of the realm that she should marry and produce an
heir to the throne; eventually, in 1650, she designated her
cousin, Charles X Gustavus, and his male descendants as the
future rulers of Sweden.

Christina's closest friend was a beautiful, young Swedish
noblewoman, Ebba Sparre, to whom she would send passionate
letters for many years before and after her abdication. Christina
also became increasingly estranged from the Lutheran Church.

On June 6, 1654, Christina renounced the throne in favor
of her cousin Charles X Gustavus in a gloomy function in the
presence of the estates of the realm in the castle of Uppsala,
ordered her valet afterward to cut her hair, and at once left
the country in male clothes under the name of Count Dohna.

Christina made a confession of the Roman Catholic faith
in Brussels and was publicly received into the church in the
Hofkirche of Innsbruck in the Tyrol; from there she set out
straight for the city of the popes. Her progress from the Alps
to Rome was a triumph. A splendid white horse, a gift from
Pope Innocent X, awaited her at the approaches to the Eternal
City. She made an impressive entry, escorted by cardinals and
pontifical noblemen, and was cheered by large crowds. The

pope ceremonially received her in St. Peter's and administered Communion to her, after which he was her host at a banquet.

The ex-queen was put up in the Vatican's Belvedere Pavillion—now a part of the pontifical museums—during her first three days in Rome. Later she resided with her little court in the Farnese Palace across the Tiber, erected more than a hundred years earlier by Cardinal Alessandro Farnese (later Pope Paul III) according to designs by famous architects, including Michelangelo. (The Palazzo Farnese today houses the French embassy to Italy.) Eventually Christina bought a palace off the right Tiber embankment, built by Cardinal Domenico Riario, which came with a pretty garden climbing the Janiculum Hill. (It is now the seat of an important national art collection.)

For more than three decades the former queen resided in Rome with only brief interruptions—in 1656 and 1657 she visited Paris and in 1660 and 1667 she returned briefly to Sweden, getting a cool reception on both occasions. It is not evident whether she managed to see her friend Ebba, who meanwhile had gotten married. During Christina's second sojourn in Paris, she ordered or engineered the assassination of her majordomo, Monaldischi, because she was convinced of his disloyalty. The murder and its motivation didn't ruffle the French authorities of the day, nor did contemporary sources seem greatly disconcerted.

When she renounced the throne, Christina had stipulated that she was entitled to a yearly appanage that would enable her to lead a dignified existence abroad. Over the years, however, the remittances from Stockholm dried up, and Christina failed to raise new money during her two trips to Sweden. Pope Alexander VII, who had succeeded Innocent X, granted the royal exile an annual allowance of twelve thousand scudi for life. Many archbishops had to live on less, but Christina would be plagued by financial worries for the rest of her days, also because her Roman household staff kept robbing her systematically and shamelessly. Pope Innocent XI, who didn't care for Christina, canceled her pension, deepening her money troubles.

Alexander VII had appointed an influential cardinal, Decio Azzolini, as the former queen's counselor, clearly expecting him to check Christina's bizarre behavior. Over the years the ex-queen and her cardinal-guardian became close friends, and Azzolini eventually lived in her palace. The Romans, of course, were convinced they were lovers, and perhaps they were. During the first years of Christina's life in Rome, other prelates were said to be smitten by her; one Cardinal Colonna made a fool of himself by his reckless courtship and by putting on makeup to look younger.

Roman gossip attributed to the former queen many lovers of either sex, especially during her first years in the city. Christina, who appeared awkward in female clothes, loved cross-dressing and was rumored to be attracted above all by pretty young nuns. Despite her scandalous reputation, she stayed in close touch with the Vatican and saw cardinals and other high churchmen almost daily. At pontifical ceremonies in St. Peter's she occupied a privileged stall near the papal altar, but might lessen the solemnity with a sotto voce remark to a neighbor and a giggle.

Christina's sardonic wit and sharp tongue were both celebrated and resented. In her old age she would say she had known four pontiffs well (Innocent X had died weeks after her arrival in Rome) but hadn't detected any common sense in any of them. She played a behind-the-scenes role in the election of four popes—Alexander VII (1655–67), Clement IX (1667–69), Clement X (1670–76), and Innocent XI (1676–89). She lobbied for one or the other of the candidates for the papacy and managed to communicate with her friend Cardinal Azzolini even though he was supposed to be sealed off from the outside world, together with the other cardinals-electors in secret conclave. The ex-queen must have felt she had become something like an unofficial member of the Sacred College of Cardinals.

As she had done in Stockholm, Christina also befriended scholars, founding a royal academy (which after her death became the prestigious Arcadian Academy).

Although chronically broke, whenever some money came Christina's way, she spent it extravagantly on her favorite of the moment. The papal court and Roman nobility had over the years grown tired of her antics and started neglecting her. In her sixties the former eminent ruler of Sweden was a short, fat, very shortsighted and bizarrely attired old lady with a double chin and a little beard, a friendly manner, and a pungent wit.

Once again she nourished Roman gossip by starting to live with an attractive, young Italian singer, Angelina Giorgini. Christina jealously guarded her latest protégée in her palace, preventing her from seeing her two lovers, a sculptor and a priest. Early in 1689 the ex-queen suddenly decided she had to see southern Italy and took her houseguest with her on the trip. Shortly after their return to Rome, Christina died of pneumonia. When her companion decamped, helped by her mother and her priestly lover, she took away from the palace what they could carry.

Pope Innocent XI, although he had detested Christina, assigned the royal convert a tomb beneath St. Peter's. She is one of the very few women whose remains rest among the sarcophagi of popes and princes in the grottoes under the pontifical altar. Christina's tomb is opposite that of Carola of Lusignano, the fifteenth-century queen of Cyprus and Jerusalem (the latter title fictitious).

II

POWERFUL VIRGIN

More than forty years with him," Mother Pascalina dreamily reminisced about Pope Pius XII when I had a long talk with her in the early 1980s. "Nuncio in Munich and Berlin, cardinal secretary of state, Holy Father." The little Bavarian nun who had wielded more influence in the Vatican than any woman in centuries was then eighty-seven years old. If I hadn't known her age, I would have guessed she was in her sixties. Her broad face with the high cheekbones and firm jaw, framed by her coif, was nearly unlined, and her dark eyes sparkled when she smiled.

Two years later, on November 13, 1983, she suddenly died in Vienna, where she had gone for a commemoration to mark the twenty-fifth anniversary of Pius XII's death. In Rome, until the last, she had been seen several times a week praying at the tomb of "her" pontiff deep below the dome of St. Peter's.

During the four decades of her association with one of the most enigmatic of modern popes, she lived under the same roof as he, kept his personal quarters in order, looked after his clothing and liturgical vestments, and served him the meals that she or some other nun had prepared. Pius XII used her also as a confidential secretary; surely she was closer to him than was any other person.

For the entire span of Pius XII's pontificate, from 1939 to 1958, Pascalina was a dominant, though mostly silent, presence on the top floor of the Vatican's Apostolic Palace and in the papal summer residence in Castel Gandolfo.

Most Romans knew of her, but very few ever saw her; even in the Vatican she could be glanced only fleetingly whenever she, in the company of other nuns, attended some solemn rite at St. Peter's, in a gallery close to the pontifical altar. Or she might be observed in the Courtyard of St. Damasus, slipping into the black Plymouth with specially made shades pulled down in the backseat windows, license plate SCV 176, for a quick errand on behalf of the pope. The driver would later tell his pals at the Vatican car pool that the German nun seemed always in a hurry and had urged him on, "Faster, faster!"

She almost never entered a curial office, but key papal officials knew the voice with the German accent well because she often relayed requests from the pontiff; whenever, exceptionally, they had to call the pope's private apartment with some urgent message, Pascalina would answer before Pius XII came on (*if* he came on).

Members of the clergy and the hierarchy at large, even archbishops and cardinals, as well as ambassadors and simple laypeople who wanted to ask Pius XII for some favor or inform him of confidential matters, often bypassed the regular channels of the Vatican bureaucracy and, instead, turned to Mother

Pascalina. If she decided to help, she could put a memo or petition on the pope's desk.

The Romans called her Pasqualina, the italianized form of her monastic name. *Pasqualina* has in the local idiom remained a synonym for a devoted, protective, and self-effacing assistant to someone in power. "Bishop [Stanislaw] Dziwisz is John Paul II's Pasqualina," Vatican insiders used to say. In the Italian press you may also read that some ambitious young aide has chosen the role of Pasqualino (the masculine form of the name) in the entourage of some politician.

During Pius XII's reign it was whispered inside the Vatican and openly said in Rome that Mother Pascalina was "the popess." As the pontiff grew older, was plagued by recurring ailments, and became increasingly withdrawn, many people said in all seriousness that the German nun was virtually running the church. To a degree she was.

Pascalina was believed to have induced Pius XII to make favorites of her bishops or cardinals. She was also credited with having been instrumental in the pontiff's decision during the church's 1950 Holy Year to formally invoke papal infallibility (as defined in 1870) to proclaim the new dogma of the Virgin Mary's bodily assumption to heaven. When during the last years of his life Pius XII confided to his closest aides that he had experienced visions of Jesus, it was generally assumed that such mystical leanings were due to Mother Pascalina's influence.

Most of the time she lived in the pontifical apartment with two other nuns of her order; the last of these were Sisters Maria Conrada Grabmair and Eswaldis Pfanner. There was no doubt, however, that Pascalina was in charge; she was addressed as "Mother," like a mother superior. It was she who sponged the pope's hands with alcohol when he came back from a mass audience during which devotees had grabbed and kissed them;

it was she who watched over the diet and schedule of her delicate and compulsively punctual master.

If a visitor had the rare privilege of being admitted to Pius XII's private quarters, Mother Pascalina would see to it that he didn't overstay his allotted time. When John Foster Dulles, President Eisenhower's secretary of state, was received by Pius XII in his personal study in 1955, the German nun appeared unasked after exactly an hour and told the visitor politely but firmly that he had to go because the Holy Father had to take dinner. The pontiff didn't say anything, and the secretary of state left. (Dulles's son Avery later became a convert to Catholicism, joined the Jesuit order, and in 2001 was made a cardinal by Pope John Paul II.)

Through the centuries most Romans have viewed the papacy with an attitude somewhere between affection and mirthful cynicism, and thus it was inevitable that Pius XII's household arrangements gave rise to many jokes. I have heard some of them also from ecclesiastics. When during the Marian Year of 1954 the Litany to Our Lady was recited in all churches, clerical wags suggested that the ritual invocation *Virgo potens!* (O powerful Virgin!) was actually addressed to Pius XII's influential housekeeper-secretary. Late in that year there were rumors in the press, eventually confirmed by the Vatican, that Jesus had appeared to the pope at the foot of his bed one morning.

"And you know what happened next?" a lay official of the Vatican told me over cappuccino at a coffee bar just outside the Gate of St. Anne. "The sovereign"—my friend always referred to the pope as "the sovereign"—"rang for Pascalina to ask her to bring two espressos instead of the usual one—the second one for his divine visitor."

Mother Pascalina much later reported in her memoirs that after Pius XII had told her of his vision that morning, she knelt and kissed the spot where he said the Savior had stood.

Rome always abounds in piquant and scandalous rumors about everybody, from the rich and mighty to your neighbor whom you meet in the elevator from time to time. Astonishingly, local gossip never came up with insinuations that there might be a sexual aspect in the long relationship between Pius XII and Pascalina; the pope just wasn't the type, the consensus was.

As a child and adolescent, the future head of the church was sickly and bookish; when he decided to become a priest he was, unusually, permitted to do most of his studies at home rather than in a seminary. Without any significant pastoral experience to his credit, the offspring of a Roman family who for generations had been associated with the Vatican in various ways entered the service of the Curia. In his early thirties, already an official at the pope's Secretariat of State, he still lived with his mother, as many no-longer-young Roman men who are not priests do to this day.

A reputation as an earnest loner followed the future pope as he rose in the church. The tall, thin, and frail-looking prelate Monsignor Eugenio Pacelli was known to have an impressive capacity for desk work and to lead an austere life because he suffered from a weak stomach. He was forty-one years old when Pope Benedict XV appointed him as apostolic nuncio—his personal ambassador—in Bavaria and consecrated him in the Sistine Chapel as a titular archbishop.

A few months after the papal diplomat had taken over his office in Munich, he had vacancies among the nunciature staff to fill; he asked the new archbishop of Munich and Freising, Michael von Faulhaber, how to go about finding replacements. The archbishop suggested turning to a Swiss German nuns' order, the Sisters Teachers of the Holy Cross of Menzingen, for help. Its provincial house at Altötting sent two of its sisters, a cook and a twenty-three-year-old teacher, Pascalina. The two nuns were told they should help out in the Munich nunciature for three months. For Pascalina the three months in Pacelli's service became forty years and seven months.

The young, pert nun, the former Josefine Lehnert, had recently completed her novitiate. She was the seventh of twelve children of a postal clerk at Ebersburg, near Munich. Pascalina reported later that since as a little girl she had been told that babies were brought by a stork that entered through the open kitchen window, she would furtively close that window at night to prevent another little sister or brother from arriving; but there was yet another baby every year. Maybe she mentioned her ineffectual method of birth control to the future pope. As Sister Pascalina (a name chosen for her by her order) she was teaching housework to girls' classes, having been prevented by the First World War from volunteering for work in some missionary district overseas.

Sister Pascalina showed much courage during the disorders in Munich after Germany's capitulation in 1918. A band of left-wing extremists, known as Spartakists, penetrated the nunciature; Archbishop Pacelli was in the hospital at the time with one of his chronic stomach complaints, but the young nun did not allow herself to be intimidated by the armed intruders. They seized the nuncio's car nevertheless.

Even then Pascalina must have already been close to the archbishop who was eighteen years older than she: he took her with him on a vacation to a house of her order at Rorschach on Lake Constance in Switzerland. The two would later spend other periods of rest in that complex, Stella Maris (Star of the Sea), which comprised a convent and a school. The grave archbishop was always an honored guest there, saying mass and conducting devotions for the nuns and their pupils.

When he was still serving in the Vatican, Pacelli, then a

sickly monsignor, had repeatedly been sent to Switzerland for rest and recovery. Italian journalists specializing in Vatican affairs have suggested that Monsignor Pacelli had first met Pascalina at the Abbey of Einsiedeln, Switzerland, when she was just eighteen years old and that years later he asked for her to be assigned to the Munich nunciature. This version is improbable. At eighteen the young Bavarian woman was still a postulant (a candidate for admission), aspiring to join the Sisters of Menzingen, an order of the Franciscan family; she would have had no business at the large Abbey of Einsiedeln, a prestigious institution of the Benedictine order.

At any rate, by 1918 in Munich, the young and pretty nun who combined religious fervor with a sense of humor and a good deal of common sense appears to have quickly become indispensable to the nuncio. Surprisingly, Pacelli entrusted Pascalina, then thirty-one years old, with the task of searching for a suitable building in Berlin and having it adapted and furnished when he became the first apostolic nuncio to Germany in 1925. Maybe the priestly diplomats on Pacelli's Munich staff were glad to have little or nothing to do with the logistics of the move. Sister Pascalina picked a villa with a garden in a distinguished section near the Tiergarten park; everybody seems to have been happy with her choice, and the Vatican approved of it.

By that time Pacelli was already fluent in German, thanks mainly to Pascalina, it seems. For the rest of his life he would speak German with Pascalina and the other nuns in his household; as a pope he (or Pascalina) gave German names to the pet birds he kept in his private quarters in the Vatican and Castel Gandolfo.

A German Jesuit, the Reverend Robert Leiber, became an adviser to the nuncio and would later serve as his secretary for special tasks in Rome. An influential priest-politician, Monsignor Ludwig Kaas, head of Germany's Zentrum Party, a Roman Catholic movement, also consulted often with the nuncio. Pacelli would later get him a Vatican job when the Zentrum was banned by Hitler; Kaas became prelate in charge of St. Peter's and the excavations underneath. Pascalina stayed in close touch with both German ecclesiastics.

Tears in the Apostolic Palace

Pacelli and Sister Pascalina were together on another working vacation in her order's Stella Maris house on Lake Constance in 1929 when Pope Pius XI nominated him as cardinal and called him back to Rome as his secretary of state. It was no surprise to anyone who knew him that he would take Sister Pascalina with him. Pius XI himself must have heard about Pacelli's housekeeper. Candidates for the cardinalate are thoroughly investigated by the Curia before the pontiff announces their elevation.

Again, the details of the move were mostly in Pascalina's hands. When the German bishops wanted to donate to the departing nuncio the furniture for his Vatican study as secretary of state, Pascalina chose the desk and other items—"valuable German woodcarving work," she would recall many years later.

The sumptuous apartment of the pope's secretary of state is on the second floor of the Apostolic Palace (the first floor to Italians), below the pope's office on the third floor. Pacelli's predecessor as secretary of state, Cardinal Pietro Gasparri, who went into retirement, vacated the premises, and Pascalina had them redone and refurnished.

Then thirty-six years old, the German nun faced formidable challenges: she spoke almost no Italian and was a stranger to the Vatican's atmosphere and culture. From morning to night she had to deal with papal officials and Vatican workers, mostly Italians. Yet she quickly learned their language and ways of doing things, and handled the job well. When the new cardinal secretary of state eventually moved from provisional quarters in the Pacelli family home near the Vatican into the official suite in the Apostolic Palace, Sister Pascalina and another member of her order had accommodations there, too.

Quite exceptionally the German nuns were allowed to stay with Cardinal Pacelli in his apartment during the election of a successor to Pius XI after his death in February 1939. The apartment was declared to be "Cell No. 13"—other participants in the conclave had to content themselves with far less comfortable "cells"—and its windows were sealed to prevent any communication with the outside world. The nuns were sworn to secrecy as "conclavists," personal attendants (usually men) to the cardinals-electors of the next pope.

There was a lot of crying in the apartment as Pacelli, after only three ballots in the Sistine Chapel, returned, already in white pontifical vestments, as Pope Pius XII and for the first time imparted the apostolic blessing on his household staff.

The scene is described in the memoirs that Mother Pascalina wrote, at the request of her order's superior, after Pius XII's death.* The proceeds from the work, which has been reissued several times, were turned over to the author's order.

The book portrays Pacelli as a prayerful, ascetic, and immensely disciplined priest who wasted no time on trivial things and worked until two A.M. every night, to be up again at six A.M. There is not one word that might be construed as criticism or less-than-reverent appraisal of Pius XII. To Pascalina, it appears, Pius XII was a saint and "one of the greatest benefactors of humankind."

---

*Sr. M. Pascalina Lehnert, *Ich durfte ihm dienen: Erinnerungen an Papst Pius XII* (Würzburg: J. W. Naumann, 1982), p. 69.

She defends him against charges that he kept silent on the Holocaust. According to Pascalina, Pius XII "was right to do in secret and without any stir all that he devised and did for saving the Jews lest he bring on them new misfortunes rather than help and salvation."

What Pascalina's memoirs contain about her own personality and feelings and her relationship with her master must be gathered by extrapolation. She clearly had a sharp eye for the funny side of people and events—even in advanced age she chuckled easily, as I found when I talked to her. During her early years with Nuncio Pacelli in Munich and Berlin and on Lake Constance, there was plenty of laughter about children and naive friars, she reports. Anyone who remembers the hieratic manner of Pius XII during his public appearances will find it difficult to imagine him laughing the way his successors Pope John XXIII, John Paul I, and John Paul II would. (Paul VI's rare smiles often seemed forced.) To conservative Roman Catholics who like to visualize the head of their church as an icon, Pius XII indeed was "the last real pope."

Whenever Pascalina quotes herself in her reminiscences, she addresses him as "Excellency" (when he was archbishop nuncio), "Eminence" (as cardinal), and "Holiness" or "Holy Father." Pacelli, it appears, started calling his housekeeper "Mother" instead of "Sister" when she was still in her thirties. Didn't he ever once call her "Pascalina" or by her baptismal name, Josefine? Wasn't there ever once in forty years an affectionate word or gesture from him or her?

Pius XII almost always ate his meals alone, served by Pascalina. At lunch his tame singing birds were let out of their cages and allowed to fly around the dining room and to the pope's table. Both he and his housekeeper were amused by their pets' capers; there is a photo of Pius XII looking fondly at his favorite canary, Gretel, which had landed on his hand. Pascalina writes that she nagged the pope about wearing an old cassock and shoes that were turning shabby, but he stubbornly kept them. Such are scenes in the cozy everyday life of long-married couples.

With a nun's roguishness, Pascalina pulled off innocent little stratagems behind her master's back. Upon her arrival in Rome, she was surprised to find that her patron in heaven, Saint Joseph, had no altar in St. Peter's. She kept urging Cardinal Pacelli to correct that slight toward the foster father of Jesus, but the secretary of state wouldn't do anything about it. So she sent a petition to his boss, Pope Pius XI (who knew her), signing it with a pseudonym. Pacelli found her out and chided her, but Pius XI was amused and Saint Joseph got his altar near the left transept of St. Peter's.

Mother Pascalina herself told me that when coal and other fuel were scarce in Rome during the war winter of 1943–44, Pius XII insisted that his quarters remain unheated like the homes of other Romans. "His hands were full of chilblains, he could hardly write or impart blessings," Pascalina reminisced. "We sisters decided we wanted some heat for him and ourselves at least on the coldest days. So we smuggled a little stove into the papal apartment; but try to heat those high-ceilinged rooms!" The pope apparently was unaware of the ineffectual ruse.

During World War II Pius XII put Mother Pascalina in charge of administering cash, food, clothing, and other things that were all the time being donated to him for his personal charities. Four storerooms in the basement of the Apostolic Palace became Pascalina's domain; she also kept two cats there and was often heard talking to them. On instructions from the pope, she would make sorties in the black Plymouth to bring aid to needy people around the city.

By that time Mother Pascalina's role and growing influence

in the Vatican were well known and possibly also exaggerated. People would write to her directly to ask for help or favors, hoping she would place their petitions "on the sacred table," the pope's desk.

Pascalina was closest to Pius XII's widowed sister, Elisabetta Rossignani, among all his relatives. During her first weeks in Rome, the German nun had lived in the Rossignani home and had started learning there some idiomatic Italian. Pius XII now and then spoke with his sister by phone but saw her as rarely as he did the other twenty or so members of the Pacelli family, except his eldest nephew, Prince Carlo Pacelli.

The Pacellis, because of their association with the Vatican over three generations, had been considered as belonging to the lower ranks of the papal (the Romans said "black") nobility. In the 1930s King Victor Emanuel III, nudged by Mussolini, bestowed on the clan the hereditary status of princes of the realm. Prince Carlo held a leading position in the administration of the State of Vatican City and in that capacity had to report to the pope from time to time; his two brothers, Prince Marcantonio and Prince Giulio Pacelli, were also Vatican dignitaries.

Despite such nepotism, Pius XII nevertheless kept his relatives at bay. A papal lay chamberlain who knew Mother Pascalina well told me that during the war, when food in Rome was hard to find, the nun successfully defended the refrigerator in the kitchen of the papal apartment against various Pacellis who tried to raid it. They particularly coveted the butter from the pontifical farm at Castel Gandolfo.

Several times the pope's sister timidly suggested to Pascalina that the Holy Father should see his relatives a little more often than he used to, but Pius XII wouldn't hear of it. Throughout his pontificate he received his family only twice a year, at Christmas and on the feast day of his heavenly patron,

Saint Eugene, on June 2. On these occasions Pascalina and the other nuns prepared and served refreshments. Each guest would find a small gift under the Christmas tree that the nuns had decorated the day before. When all were assembled, the pope would appear, talk to each one, ask how the children were doing in school, give them all the apostolic blessing, which they received on their knees, and withdraw again. He was never one for small talk. There are nevertheless hints in Mother Pascalina's memoirs that she may have gently teased him from time to time or brought up everyday matters.

Like many devoted wives who have been married for a long time, Pascalina appeared to feel that the otherworldly pope couldn't do without her. In 1954 she slipped on the marble floor of the pontifical apartment and broke a leg. She was taken to the Salvator Mundi International Hospital on the Janiculum Hill but would stay for only a few days. Soon she was back on the top floor of the Apostolic Palace, cruising around the pontifical quarters in a wheelchair. Heaps of flowers kept arriving at the fashionable clinic on the Janiculum, run by the Sisters of the Divine Savior, where she had been treated; Pascalina sent word that they should all be placed in the hospital's chapel. High prelates and diplomats were among those to whom she sent thank-you notes.

Sentinel Nun

Curial officials found that access to Pius XII often depended on being in Pascalina's good graces. Visitors from Germany whom she had known when the pope was nuncio in Munich or Berlin quickly obtained an audience with him; others had to wait or didn't get a chance to speak with him at all. Even cardinals were well advised to cultivate the German nun, and quite a few did.

One of her favorites was Cardinal Francis Spellman, the powerful archbishop of New York who had worked with Pacelli in the Secretariat of State when both were just monsignors. Whenever Cardinal Spellman visited the Vatican, which was relatively often, Pius XII asked him to dinner, an exceptional honor. On such occasions Mother Pascalina and the other nuns cooked pasta, which the Rome-trained American cardinal loved. One of the gifts that Spellman brought the pope was a newfangled contraption, an electric razor. From then on Pius XII was usually badly shaved.

The dean of the Sacred College of Cardinals, Eugene Tisserant, above all bristled at Pascalina's increasingly influential behind-the-scenes role. Tisserant, tall and bearded, had once been a French officer in Syria; he was a learned and forceful expert on Middle Eastern affairs. As the ranking senior cardinal—the dean is not necessarily the eldest of his brethren—he was entitled to certain privileges, including almost automatic access to the pontiff. During the last years of Pius XII's life, Pascalina sometimes sent word to the dean of cardinals that the pope couldn't receive him because he was unwell. The proud French prince of the church would not forget such perceived affronts from the German nun.

Cardinal Tisserant and other curialists as well as diplomats also gave to understand they found it odd that German was the lingua franca in the papal household even during World War II. In addition to the German nuns, there was Father Leiber; as private secretary (although he was increasingly plagued by asthma); he had an office of his own beneath the papal apartment. Another German Jesuit, the Reverend Augustin Bea, served as the pope's confessor and unofficial counselor. Father Bea, then a professor at the Pontifical Bible

Institute, was later to emerge as a leading ecumenicist at the Second Vatican Council (1962–65); Pope John XXIII would make him a cardinal. Bea would take the lead in framing the epochal council document *Nostra Aetate* (In This Age of Ours), which absolved the Jewish people of the old accusation of being responsible for the crucifixion of Jesus.

Monsignor Kaas, who had once played a leading part in German politics, would also see Pius XII frequently; he periodically informed the pontiff regarding the progress of the archaeologists' search for the burial place of the Apostle Peter in the excavations below the basilica dedicated to him.

Within Pius XII's closest entourage there was some tension: a permanent feud carried out with pointed remarks and unpleasant little attitudes was going on between Mother Pascalina and the pope's valet-driver, Giovanni Antinori. The rotund Antinori, who saw his master daily, lived with his family within Vatican City. He appears to have been the main source of gossip about the "third floor," the private quarters of the pope, which was secured—as it is also today—around the clock by Swiss Guardsmen.

Of Pius XII's two closest aides in governing the church, Pascalina liked Monsignor Domenico Tardini much better than Monsignor Giovanni Battista Montini (who was later to become Pope Paul VI). They headed the two main divisions of the Secretariat of State—one in charge of internal church affairs, the other mainly concerned with its external relations. After the death of Cardinal Luigi Maglione, Pius XII's colorless first secretary of state (and his successor in that position), the pontiff did not replace him. For the remaining fourteen years of his reign, he ran the show personally with the help of the two workhorse prelates, Tardini and Montini. The two usually saw the pope separately once or twice every day and spoke with him (or with Mother Pascalina) by phone between their face-to-face meetings.

Tardini, who was eventually to become cardinal secretary of state under Pope John XXIII, was outgoing, could be cordial or choleric, and wasn't above cracking a joke now and then. Pascalina mentions him often in her memoirs. Montini, whose personality somewhat resembled Pius XII's, was never seen to laugh. Cardinal Benelli, who for years had been a close aide to Montini, told me: "He was heroic in his sense of duty. Imagine, for years and years he would answer Pius XII's frequent phone calls, day and night, no later than after the second ring."

In 1954, Pius XII surprisingly appointed Montini arch-bishop of Milan, although it was known that he would have much preferred to stay on in the Vatican. Pascalina was sus-pected to have had a hand in the transfer. Even more aston-ishing was that during the last four years of his pontificate, Pius XII failed to make Montini a cardinal—although as the head of one of the world's largest archdioceses, the incumbent could expect to receive the red hat almost by right. John XXIII quickly made up for the apparent snub, raising Montini to the cardinalate and thus making him eligible for eventual election to the papacy. Pascalina refers to Montini in her book only once, fleetingly.

The German nun distrusted Pius XII's personal physician, Riccardo Galeazzi-Lisi, and the doctor was known to detest her. Pascalina's instincts were clamorously vindicated after the pope's death. It was discovered that Galeazzi-Lisi had for years sold medical information regarding his illustrious patient to the media and had surreptitiously taken pictures of the dying pope for *Paris Match* magazine. Disgraced, Galeazzi-Lisi lost his Vat-ican position as "pontifical archiater" (chief physician) and was ousted from the Italian Medical Association. Many years later when I brought up the affair during a talk with Mother Pascalina, she changed the topic. In her book she only refers to "the doctor" without ever mentioning his name.

When Pius XII's health deteriorated in his last years and he was periodically tormented by long spells of hiccuping, Pascalina brought in a Swiss gerontologist, Paul Niehans. The Swiss treated the pontiff with his controversial "living cell" therapy, injecting finely ground tissue taken from freshly slaughtered lambs. Apparently convinced that the treatment was successful, Pius XII appointed Dr. Niehans, a Protestant, to the Pontifical Academy of Sciences, an international Vatican body, to take over the seat that had become vacant by the death in 1953 of Sir Alexander Fleming, the discoverer of penicillin. Doctors Niehans and Galeazzi-Lisi made no secret of the low opinion they had of each other.

During Pius XII's last illness he was treated by well-regarded Roman physicians in addition to Dr. Galeazzi-Lisi. On Pascalina's insistence, Dr. Niehans too was summoned to Castel Gandolfo, although the Italian medical establishment considered him a quack. In her memoirs Pascalina asserts that the Swiss doctor "never left [the pope's] sickbed." He must have, though, from time to time; otherwise, Dr. Galeazzi-Lisi could have had no chance of photographing the agonizing patient. As if to compound his ignominy, the archiater bungled the embalming of Pius XII's remains, thus hastening his own downfall.

Challenging a Cardinal

The pope had not yet expired at Castel Gandolfo when Cardinal Tisserant had the pontifical study in the Vatican sealed. The French dean of the Sacred College of Cardinals acted legitimately in his capacity as cardinal camerlengo (chamberlain), the Vatican official responsible for proceedings during the

Vacancy of the See, from the death and burial of a pontiff until the election of his successor.

When Pius XII had been officially pronounced dead, Tisserant asked Mother Pascalina for the pope's personal papers. She told the dean of cardinals that on the pontiff's oft-repeated orders, she had burned three baskets full of notes, most of them handwritten, when his condition had taken a turn for the worse. At the time I was told by various people who had been at Castel Gandolfo that there had been a bitter confrontation between the nun and the cardinal.

Tisserant upbraided Mother Pascalina for having destroyed a historical treasure that should have been turned over to the Secretariat of State and eventually to the Vatican's Secret Archives. The nun is supposed to have replied, yes, she had burned three bags of documents but she had received the Holy Father's specific order to do so in case he hadn't time to burn them himself. "All my life I have obeyed; a pope's order must be carried out. Your Eminence, would you have done otherwise?" Pascalina did tell Cardinal Tisserant where Pius XII's will was to be found, namely in a drawer of his desk in his Vatican apartment, produced the key to it, and was present when the cardinal retrieved the document.

Cardinal Tisserant ordered Pascalina and the other two nuns of Pius XII's household to get together their things from their quarters in Castel Gandolfo and the Vatican's Apostolic Palace and clear out. Carrying four birdcages with Pius XII's pets and small bundles with their own personal belongings, the nuns soon arrived in a Vatican car at the Pontifical North American College on the Janiculum Hill, which Pius XII had inaugurated a few years earlier. Cardinal Spellman, who knew how fortunes in the Vatican may change, had repeatedly told Pascalina that if she or other members of her order were ever to need a place to stay in Rome, they would be welcome at the North American College.

Many graduates of that institution, which trains Americans for the priesthood, remember the friendly German nun who sought to make herself useful at the college, every day went to pray at Pius XII's tomb in the grottoes of nearby St. Peter's, and would put flowers in the room of seminarians on the feast day of their patron saint.

But the energetic Mother Pascalina was also working on a project of her own. She obtained the use of a sloping plot of land on the Monte Mario, a hill on Rome's northern outskirts, and tirelessly raised funds to build a rest home for elderly women. The place, Pastor Angelicus House, was opened in 1962 and is operated by her order. It was there that I spoke to Mother Pascalina for nearly two hours. I had written to her, asking to see her, and she promptly called me at home and in a clear, strong voice set a date.

During our talk she told me that the Congregation for the Causes of the Saints, the department of the Curia in charge of preparing beatifications and canonizations, had by then questioned her thirty-three times as a key witness in the canonical process that was to determine whether Pius XII had had the "heroic virtues" qualifying him to be proclaimed "blessed" and, eventually, a saint. She must have been a friendly witness.

Mother Pascalina also recalled her first audience with Pius XII's successor, Pope John XXIII. "His Holiness took me around the entire pontifical apartment," she said, "and I noticed that hardly anything had been changed. The Holy Father asked me who had donated certain pictures on the walls, and I of course could tell him."

It seems that Pope Paul VI, who succeeded John XXIII, didn't care to have his private quarters inspected by Mother Pascalina. As Monsignor Montini and aide to Pius XII, he had

been in the pontifical apartment innumerable times and had
seen Mother Pascalina almost daily; there had never been anything more than formal politeness between them. When Montini, then archbishop of Milan, became pope, he had the
staterooms and the pontifical suite above them redecorated by
Milanese architects and artists. Pastel yellows, beige, and champagne hues now prevailed; damask draperies and gilt wood were
supplanted by sober modern curtains and chairs. Baroque religious art made room for Gothic and early-Renaissance paintings and sculptures. The massive wooden furniture that the
German bishops had given Cardinal Pacelli was thrown out
and replaced by teak.

Pope John Paul II did ask Mother Pascalina, then in her
eighties, to see him in his private quarters. "The Holy Father
was very kind to me and showed me how the place is now,"
she told me. She wouldn't say if she liked the new look.

After her death in Vienna in 1983, Mother Pascalina was
buried in the small cemetery of the 1,300-year-old German
College inside Vatican City, the Campo Santo Teutonico.

Her grave, facing the college's church, is covered on ground
level with a broad travertine slab. A German inscription reads,
in translation:

> WE ARE AWAITING THE RESURRECTION
> SISTERS OF THE HOLY CROSS OF MENZINGEN
> SISTER PASCALINA LEHNERT
> AUGUST 13, 1894–NOVEMBER 13, 1983

The grave is adorned with pink and purple potted flowers,
as are many of the other graves and elaborate tombs in the
historic cemetery. A directory near the entrance to the church
states that Sister Pascalina was for many years in the service
of Pope Pius XII, later was mother superior of a community of

her order at the Pontifical North American College in Rome, and eventually founded the Pastor Angelicus House, a rest home for aged women.

Mother Pascalina's grave was apparently destined to receive also the remains of other members of her order, but she is the only one buried there. Her resting place in the old cemetery south of the left transept of St. Peter's is only a few yards away from Pius XII's tomb in the grottoes beneath the basilica where she prayed so often.

In the days immediately after Pius XII's death, I heard from various people who had been in Castel Gandolfo that Mother Pascalina had embraced the defunct's feet and was heard to murmur amid sobs: "I'll see you in heaven." The anecdote may be sentimental fiction, but it is likely to reflect her feelings.

III

SCHOLARSHIP AND SANCTITY

Since the death of Pope Pius XII, no woman has exercised influence in the Vatican comparable to the conspicuous backstage (or upstairs) role that Mother Pascalina played for so long. Very important to the papacy nevertheless was the work of a female scholar, Margherita Guarducci (1902–99), whom the German nun liked and admired.

An epigraphist and archaeologist of international renown, Professor Guarducci supplied new scientific arguments to support the popes' ancient assertion that the Apostle Peter was buried beneath what is now the mighty basilica consecrated to him.

Some critics of Catholicism over the centuries have contended that the Apostle Peter was never in Rome. Martin Luther conceded the apostle's presence in the city of the emperors but wrote that nobody knew where he had been laid to rest.

The assumption that the Prince of the Apostles came to the center of the Roman empire, was the first bishop of Rome, and was buried in the Vatican is the basis for the popes' claim to primacy in the Christian church as successors of Saint Peter. Professor Guarducci was convinced that she had found conclusive proof justifying that claim, and she convinced the pontiffs.

A native of Florence, Margherita Guarducci studied at the old University of Bologna and did postgraduate work in Greece and Germany. She explored Greek inscriptions on the island of Crete, resulting in a four-volume report. For more than four decades she taught Greek epigraphy and antiquities at Rome State University La Sapienza. She was a member of Italian and foreign scientific academies, and in addition to several books she wrote four hundred magazine articles and scholarly papers.

She joined the small team that was probing the subsoil beneath St. Peter's fifteen years after the excavations started. The Emperor Constantine had the first Basilica of St. Peter erected in the fourth century on the site—the Vatican—where the apostle's burial place was presumed to be. The current Basilica of St. Peter, built in the sixteenth century, occupies the same location. Through the centuries the faithful have been convinced that the apostle's tomb was directly beneath the papal altar over which Michelangelo elevated his triumphant dome.

Awe had prevented any deep digging underneath the altar. Excavations started only after Pope Pius XI, who died in 1939, in his will expressed the desire to be buried near the tomb of Saint Peter. The excavations were carried out by the maintenance crew of St. Peter's, whom the Romans call the *sampietrini*, under the direction of Professor Enrico Josi, a papal official and expert on early Christian catacombs; Bruno M. Apolloni Ghetti, an architect; and two Jesuit archaeologists, Fathers Antonio Ferrua and Engelbert Kirschbaum. The entire

operation was supervised by Monsignor Ludwig Kaas, the former leader of the German Zentrum Party, in his capacity as
prelate in charge of St. Peter's.

The Bones of Saint Peter

For ten years very little was known about what was going on
deep below St. Peter's. The *New York Times* was the first newspaper in the world to report that the archaeologists were convinced they had located Saint Peter's tomb. Pope Pius XII in
his Christmas message at the end of the 1950 Holy Year said:
"Has the tomb of Saint Peter really been found? . . . Yes, the
tomb of the Prince of the Apostles has been found."

What actually had come to light was a pagan cemetery near
the Circus of Emperor Nero in which, according to ancient
Christian tradition, Saint Peter was crucified. During the first
decades of the Christian era, adherents of the new faith, too,
were buried in the old cemetery. One of the Christian graves
was more conspicuous than the others, and a little shrine was
built over it during the middle of the second century. Graffiti
had been scratched into nearby walls. Among Greek and Latin
words, the Greek monogram of Christ, *khi* and *rho* superim-
posed, recurred. The archaeologists were certain the graffiti
were the work of early Christians who had worshiped at the
tomb of Saint Peter.

When Professor Guarducci saw the first reproductions of
some of the graffiti, she asked Pope Pius XII (who already knew
her) in writing to be permitted to examine the originals. Her
request was granted; she joined the excavation team in 1952.
For several years she descended below St. Peter's on the three
mornings every week when she wasn't lecturing at the university. At the excavation site she usually worked kneeling on the

earth floor to see the graffiti at eye level; in her left hand she held a flashlight and tried to write with her right, the notepad on her knee.

During those years I twice interviewed Professor Guarducci. She then lived with her adoring and protective sister in a musty old palazzo on the Via della Scrofa, not far from the Pantheon and a half-hour walk from the Vatican. Then in her late fifties, she was slim and agile, a forceful academic personage. I thought, *I'm glad I don't have to take an exam before her.*

Professor Guarducci soon found that the four male excavation experts were distrustful and jealous of one another, and quickly also of her. The two Jesuits, one Italian and the other German, seemed especially antagonistic. The Italian took a piece of masonry with a crucial inscription to his convent, and it required the intervention of the pope and the superior general of the Society of Jesus to get him to return the important fragment to St. Peter's.

Many of the first Christians in ancient Rome were Greek-speaking immigrants (the Gospels were written in Greek). Professor Guarducci deciphered one of the Greek graffiti as "Peter is in here." Other inscriptions were, according to her, scratchings in what she called "magic cryptography"—writing in a secret code with religious meanings—to evade anti-Christian persecution. She personally reported on her findings to Popes Pius XII, John XXIII, and Paul VI in many audiences.

Ancient Roman coins and fragments of human bones were also found at the excavation site. Professor Guarducci determined that the coins were votive offerings by early Christians. The bones had been long neglected by the diggers. Eventually the Vatican called in an anthropologist, Venerando Correnti of the Universities of Palermo and Rome, charging him with analyzing the fragments.

Professor Correnti concluded that the bones were the remains of various persons, male and female; it appeared that one group of bones belonged to a robust man between sixty and seventy years of age. Pondering all the archaeological, epigraphical, and anthropological data, Professor Guarducci became convinced that some of the bone fragments in question were remains of Saint Peter. On November 25, 1963, she reported to Pope Paul VI that the bones of the apostle had been identified "with extreme probability."

Paul VI authorized Professor Guarducci to submit a report on her work to a small group of experts. News of her claim to have identified Saint Peter's bones inevitably leaked out, stirring scientific controversy. Guarducci's thesis was received with skepticism by several Vatican officials as well as by nonreligious scholars. When she read a paper on her explorations in a 1965 session of the Accademia dei Lincei, an eminent learned society in Rome of which she was a member, an authoritative Italian historian, Luigi Salvatorelli (1886–1974), who was in the audience loudly harrumphed. One of the two Jesuit archaeologists of the excavation team, Father Ferrua, also dissented from his female colleague.

Yet on June 26, 1968, Pope Paul VI in a general audience in the Vatican announced that "the relics of Saint Peter have been identified in a way that we may consider convincing."

One day later, almost the eve of the feast of Saint Peter and Saint Paul (June 29), the relics were returned to the tomb deep below the papal altar whence they had been removed by Monsignor Kaas (who died in 1952) twenty-seven years earlier. A formal document recording the restitution was signed by a cardinal, seven ecclesiastical and lay Vatican officials, and Professor Guarducci as the sole woman witness.

Unlike Professor Guarducci, the handful of international female experts whom the popes have lately appointed to the Pontifical Academy of Sciences cannot properly be described as women of the Vatican. They have barely any influence on Holy See affairs or papal teachings. The four-hundred-year-old academy is made up of eighty members who meet from time to time in the graceful Renaissance Villa of Pope Paul IV in the Vatican Gardens or who take part in smaller symposiums in the fields of mathematical and experimental sciences. It's a prestige thing for both the Vatican and the academy members. They are addressed as "your excellency" by Vatican officials.

The pontifical academicians are named by the pope for life, regardless of their faith or absence of faith, nationality, or gender. The current membership includes various Nobel laureates. An Italian in the group, Rita Levi-Montalcini, co-winner of the 1986 Nobel prize for physiology and medicine, is Jewish and has occasionally made public statements contradicting the Vatican's stance on various issues.

From the late twentieth century some women have attained high-level positions in academic institutions affiliated with the Vatican. Thus, the secretary general of the Pontifical Gregorian University is currently an unwed laywoman, Barbara Bergami. At the Lateran University the dean of the philosophy department is a married woman, Professor Angela Ales Bello.

Female diplomats accredited to the Holy See belong, in a sense, to the flock of the Vatican's women. They regularly meet with officials of the papal Secretariat of State, see cardinals and other prelates at receptions and dinner parties, and attend ceremonies in St. Peter's in front seats; they may even have a private audience with the pope once in a while.

Lately a few nations have assigned female diplomats not only as counselors, but also as ambassadors to the Holy See. Panama, Paraguay, the Philippines, South Africa, and Ukraine, among others, sent women as mission chiefs. The U.S. embassy to the Vatican was headed from 1997 to 2001 by Corinne (Lindy) Boggs, a former ten-time representative for Louisiana in Congress. In her early eighties, Mrs. Boggs with her New Orleans charm was a great success in Rome's diplomatic and clerical society; elderly archbishops were flattered when she addressed them as "dahlin'."

Saint in a Sari

It is tempting to include also Mother Teresa of Calcutta (1910–97) among the Vatican's women. True, whenever Pope Paul VI or Pope John Paul II received the sari-clad, stooped, and wrinkled nun in audience, she looked uneasy with her quizzical half smile amid the ripe Roman splendor; yet with her immense worldwide prestige, she strenuously supported the papacy's conservative views on birth control and abortion. The Vatican owed her much gratitude.

As the recipient of the 1979 Nobel Peace Prize, Mother Teresa in her acceptance speech in Oslo in the presence of King Olav V of Norway and the diplomatic corps bluntly expressed sorrow for nations (like Norway) that had legalized abortion: "They fear the little ones, fear the unborn children. . . . We are fighting abortion with adoptions."

Mother Teresa herself was born into an ethnic Albanian Catholic middle-class family in Skopje in 1910, technically a subject of the sultan in Istanbul. Turkey lost the city along with a large chunk of Macedonia, to Serbia in 1912. Skopje is now the capital of the independent republic of Macedonia. Gonxha Bojaxhiu, the future Mother Teresa, would successively become a citizen of Serbia, Yugoslavia, and eventually India. She was an attractive graduate of Skopje High School when, at the age of eighteen, she announced to the astonishment of her mother, brother, and sister that she wanted to become a missionary nun.

She entered the Institute of the Blessed Virgin Mary, better known as the Loretto Sisters, and after a few months in their Dublin, Ireland, convent was sent to Darjeeling, India, for her novitiate. As Sister Teresa, she first stayed in that resort in the Himalaya foothills and eventually was assigned to a teaching post at her order's St. Mary's High School for girls from affluent families in Calcutta, some 430 miles to the south. Ultimately she became the school's principal. During those years she also learned to speak fluent Bengali and Hindi.

As Mother Teresa herself has told it, she reached the decision to abandon her relatively comfortable life as an educator in an elite institution to personally take care of Calcutta's poorest people during a night journey in an Indian railroad train in 1946.

She petitioned her mother superior, the archbishop of Calcutta, and the Vatican for permission to leave the Loretto Sisters and found her own community of religious women dedicated to the apostolate in the slums. Her request was granted, and she attended nursing and midwifery courses conducted by the American Medical Missionary Sisters in Patna on the Ganges. Then she embarked on her own, seeking out the homeless, the sick, the dying, the abandoned children, and the lepers in Calcutta's appalling districts of misery.

Soon some young Indian women, mostly former students of hers, joined Mother Teresa. They all dressed in the white sari of the poor, and eventually took over a three-story house next to a temple of Kali, the Hindu goddess of death, at 54A Lower Circular Road, Calcutta, that a Muslim who was leaving for Pakistan had sold them cheaply. In 1950 Mother Teresa formally set up her congregation, Carriers of Christ's Love in the Slums, later officially known as Missionaries of Charity.

That modest building has seen more than sixty thousand sick, destitute, and dying people. Prelates, priests, members of the laity, writers, and journalists have visited it as well as vol-

unteers who stayed awhile to work under Mother Teresa's no-
nonsense direction. She impressed them all with her
unsentimental practicality, her organizational skills, her deep
piety, and her talent for saving money and raising funds. At
predawn mass at her headquarters she might appear mystically
absorbed in prayer but would suddenly get up to turn off the
lights in the chapel because sunrise had made them unneces-
sary.

Missionaries of Charity grew and spread outside India.
Non-Indian women started enrolling; the congregation's common language remained English. Mother Teresa stayed close to
the Jesuits who were influential in her original order, the Loretto Sisters. The sight of a pair of nuns—they usually don't
walk alone in the streets—in white saris bordered with blue
stripes became familiar in many cities everywhere.

In 1968 Mother Teresa received a personal letter from Pope
Paul VI with two airline tickets from Calcutta to Rome and a
check for $10,000. The pontiff was asking her to establish a
Missionaries of Charity house in the Italian capital, where, he
wrote, its poor were sadly neglected. Mother Teresa flew to
Rome with one of her sisters and chose a building in a seedy
neighborhood near a ruined ancient Roman aqueduct as her
base. There she opened a center for ambulatory medical treatment and day care, and assigned qualified members of her congregation to it. The "Indian sisters," as they are fondly called
locally, now also operate other outposts in Rome, including a
hostel for the homeless not far from the central railroad terminal and another one in the neighborhood of the Vatican.

Mother Teresa's nuns soon started appearing in North
America. In New York they installed themselves in a former
convent in the South Bronx, and in 1985 they opened a house
for AIDS patients in Manhattan with support from the archbishop of New York, the late Cardinal John J. O'Connor. One

of the first Roman Catholic organizations to focus on AIDS victims, Missionaries of Charity became active in this field also in Haiti and in Latin American, African, and Asian countries.

When Mother Teresa was eighty years old in 1990, she resigned as general superior of her order but continued caring for the sick, the dying, and poor children. Before and after receiving the Nobel Peace Prize, Mother Teresa won many other awards and honors, using the attendant money for her congregation. She traveled a lot, gave countless interviews, and in effect became the second-best-known public-relations personality of the Roman Catholic Church (after Pope John Paul II).

Unavoidably there was also criticism of Mother Teresa's restless activities. She was blamed for her unquestioning endorsement of the Vatican's bans on abortion and artificial birth control. (She did accept the "rhythm method" of periodic sexual abstinence.) She was also accused of remaining silent on the political, economic, and social causes of the world's big-city ills.

In the Vatican Mother Teresa was treated with something like awe during her brief visits. Living with her nuns in their modest quarters, she would take the public bus to reach St. Peter's Square, where the Swiss Guards snapped to attention, presenting their halberds to her. Papal officials bowed deep, and cardinals showed respect for the slight old nun in her sari. In 1985 Pope John Paul II asked her to address the bishops' synod, a periodic consultative assembly in the Vatican. She far exceeded the time allotted to synod speakers, but nobody cut her off. She had in fact been acknowledged as the Vatican's most important woman.

Mother Teresa had also become a formidable media personality. Toward the end of her life another darling of the world's press and TV, Princess Diana of Britain, visited with her, professing admiration for her work and apparently seeking her friendship. The two women, each endowed with a charisma all her own, died within a week of each other. India decreed a state funeral for the Albanian-born nun who had always professed to be an Indian. Pope John Paul II sent his secretary of state, Cardinal Angelo Sodano, as his personal representative to the burial.

Two days after Mother Teresa's death of a heart attack, John Paul II paid tribute to her in an address to pilgrims at Castel Gandolfo. "This nun who was universally recognized as Mother of the Poor was an enduring example for all, believers and nonbelievers," the pontiff declared. With an allusion to her stand on birth control and abortion, the pope stressed that "in the great heart of Mother Teresa a special place was reserved for the family."

At latest count, the Missionaries of Charity have 615 houses with 4,400 sisters in more than a hundred countries. Their headquarters is still in Mother Teresa's original base in Calcutta; the order now runs scores of centers in the greater Calcutta area. An Indian sister is the congregation's superior general.

The consensus in the Vatican is that Mother Teresa will soon be declared to be "blessed" and eventually be proclaimed a saint in a solemn canonization rite. Pope John II authorized the Curia to speed up the procedure for her beatification. By mid-2001 the canonical examination of her life and works on the diocesan level—which usually takes at least five years—had been completed. Testimony gathered in Calcutta and elsewhere filled 34,000 pages in seventy-six volumes, and there were already reports of miracles attributed to Mother Teresa's heavenly intercession. Chances are that the Vatican will recognize her as a saint in record time.

IV

THE PURPLE CEILING

If you were a man, you'd be at least a bishop," I suggested to an American nun, one of the highest-ranking women in the Roman Curia.

"Well, maybe a monsignor," she replied with a smile.

Monsignors, of whom there are hundreds in the Vatican, rank below bishops but above mere priests and friars in the intricate pecking order of the Roman Catholic Church. Prelates—a term applicable to anyone from monsignor to cardinal—are as keenly conscious of their position in the hierarchy as are captains or generals in the military, even though the distinguished clerics may make a show of modesty and wear a plain Roman collar in everyday life rather than display the purple or crimson of their station.

It was at a small lunch in the home of a curial archbishop who would soon become a cardinal that I first met the female

Vatican official; there was also a multilingual Irish monsignor (a year later he was a bishop) and a learned Jesuit, both on the staff of the Curia, the bureaucratic arm of the papacy. A lot of curial give-and-take occurs at table.

Had I seen the nun on the street or in a bus, I wouldn't have guessed her affiliation. In her sixties, fresh-faced and gray-haired, she wore a decorous dark blue suit with a below-the-knee skirt; there was just a little cross, which any layperson might sport, too. She later told me that she was living with two sisters of her congregation in an apartment near the Lateran, a kind of miniconvent.

Our host's comfortable apartment, which included a private chapel and broad terraces, was on the top floor of a condominium on Rome's western outskirts, a ten-minute car ride from St. Peter's. We were served by a middle-aged Asian woman who had also cooked the very Roman meal—pasta al dente, veal cutlets, salad, and a cake; there was a carafe of red wine. Our host said grace before we tackled the spaghetti.

The archbishop's housekeeper wore a large wooden cross over her smock; she was probably a member of some religious order or society. In a gesture of monastic sisterliness, the American nun at one point got up and went into the kitchen to help, and we heard the two women chatting and chuckling. It is good form for nuns to show familiarity with housework.

Having learned that the American nun was traveling far and wide on a Holy See service passport to represent the Vatican at international events, I compared notes with her on airport-hopping in Africa. When she recalled trips to Cairo and Beijing as a member of Vatican delegations, I made that remark about doing a bishop's job.

At the United Nations Conference on Population and Development in Cairo in 1994, the Vatican representatives managed to defeat a broad pro-abortion front formed by many governments and to some extent supported by the Clinton administration. The papal delegation used obstructionist tactics to keep language advocating abortion out of the conference resolutions.

At the United Nations Conference on Women in Beijing in 1995, the Vatican delegation restated the church's rejection of abortion but also called for equal rights for women in the fields of education and employment. Shouldn't a woman employee of the papal government also be able to attain the rank of bishop?

Bishops, in several branches of Christianity, are considered successors of the Twelve Apostles. The twelve were all men, which is the reason adduced by the Roman Catholic Church and certain other Christian denominations for excluding women from the priesthood.

However, the Gospels report that in addition to the apostles, many women were around Jesus. In particular, he was followed from Galilee to Jerusalem by Mary Magdalen and other female devotees who then witnessed the Crucifixion and were the first to alert the male disciples to the Resurrection. After the Ascension of Jesus his mother, Mary, and "the women" stayed together in Jerusalem with the apostles and other male disciples (Acts 1:14).

The great number of sainted virgins and matrons, as well as female martyrs, attests to the conspicuous role of pious women in early Christianity. Yet Saint Paul wrote to the Corinthians that "women must keep silent in the church" (1 Cor. 14:34). And in his Epistle to Timothy, the apostle repeated: "I suffer not a woman to teach, nor use authority over the men but to be in silence" (1 Tim. 2:12). However, in his Epistle to the Galatians, Saint Paul proclaimed the equality of Christians of either sex: "There is neither Jew nor Greek, there is neither slave nor free, there is neither male nor female. For you are all one in Christ Jesus" (Gal. 3:28).

Roman Catholicism's calendar of saints comprises more women than men; the ratio is about three to two. Pope John Paul II canonized many female saints, including (in 1998) Saint Edith Stein, the Jewish-born philosopher who became a Carmelite nun and died in the concentration camp of Auschwitz in 1942. A new parish church on Rome's eastern outskirts has been dedicated to her, and the Polish pontiff visited it in May 2001 to say mass.

During the first Christian millennium many priests were married, and many still are married today in Eastern Christian communities, some of whom recognize the primacy of the pope in Rome. The Second Vatican Council (Vatican II, 1962–65) admitted in its Decree on the Ministry and Life of Priests that "celibacy is not demanded of the priesthood by its nature." The decree concedes that the Eastern churches have "many excellent married priests." Vatican II also reintroduced the ancient Christian ministry of deacons, who may be married and assist the priests, or substitute for them, in certain liturgical functions.

Obligatory celibacy was sternly enforced in the Western church by Pope Saint Gregory VII (1073–85) and his successors. Gregory, earlier known as Hildebrand, a combative Benedictine monk from Tuscany, himself depended on the support of one of the most powerful female figures of the Middle Ages, the Lombard-descended Matilda of Tuscia (Tuscany) in the ecclesiastical and political quarrels in which he was continually embroiled. In one of her castles, at Canossa (near Bologna), Emperor Henry IV humbled himself by kneeling in the snow one winter day in 1077 to do penance before the pope who, at the side of Matilda, was looking on from a window. Six years later Henry IV had his revenge: he conquered Rome and forced the pope into exile. Gregory VII died in Salerno and is buried in the cathedral there; his ban on married priests has survived to this day.

During the early 1990s the Vatican bureaucracy was still reluctant to allow female pre-teenagers to serve as acolytes at mass even though altar girls were by then already a fairly common sight in Roman Catholic churches in the United States and elsewhere—even in some suburban parishes in the pope's own diocese, Rome. Currently women read Scripture passages and inspirational texts at some masses; nuns take Communion—the host consecrated by a priest—to sick people in their homes; and female parish assistants share pastoral tasks with male clergy.

The Vatican itself was never an all-male domain the way the Orthodox monks' community at Mount Athos in northeastern Greece—virtually an autonomous enclave—is; all females, human or animal, are banned there. In the papal palaces some nuns and other women have always been around, if only for workaday chores. Some popes have had female advisers, such as Saint Catherine of Siena in the fourteenth century or Mother Teresa in the twentieth.

A few pontiffs kept mistresses—Alexander VI had at least six children by them—no fewer than four by Vannozza de Cataneis, including the beautiful Lucrezia Borgia.

Nobody in the Curia today likes to be reminded of the embarrassments of the Renaissance. The ambience in the sacred palaces has indeed become austere during the last few centuries even though popes and prelates have had and continue to have female housekeepers.

Female Infiltration

The number of women in the Vatican has greatly increased since the middle of the twentieth century. Nuns and laywomen started working in curial offices as secretaries, accountants, ar-

chivists, computer operators, and translators; a few even attained slightly higher positions. The Vatican Museums and
Vatican Radio hired qualified women. Handpicked nuns and
some female academics and professional women were given
consultative functions in departments of the Curia that brought
them to Rome from time to time.

When the Vatican searched for some credible female representative to head its official delegation to the 1995 women's
conference in Beijing, it found none among its own personnel
and had to ask a relative outsider, Mary Ann Glendon of Harvard University, to take on the job. Professor Glendon was at
the time a member of the Pontifical Academy of Social Sciences, a body that meets in Rome every now and then. She
was later entrusted with other consultative curial positions.

As of the summer of 2002, not quite one-tenth of the Vatican workforce of three thousand is female. Add to them the
wives and daughters of papal lay staff who have living quarters
in Vatican City, and the women—mostly nuns—who serve as
housekeepers of the pope, cardinals, and lesser prelates living
in papal buildings.

Most of the Vatican's women employees, nuns, and female
members of the laity know one another, at least by sight, from
religious ceremonies they attend or from more mundane encounters. Is there a chance for networking in the Vatican,
something like a female caucus? I asked a nun who works in
the Curia's human rights division. "It would be counterproduc-
tive," she said. "Our ecclesiastic superiors, many of whom were
negatively impressed by the rhetoric of early feminism, always
suspect we want to be priests. We don't. If there existed some
horizontal grouping of women at the Holy See, those suspicions
would be reinforced."

I have heard that phrase, "we don't want to be priests," several times from different nuns over the years—so often, indeed,

that it eventually sounded to me like a knee-jerk defense to ward off clerical distrust. The subtext: We are not uppity, though we shouldn't mind to do a priest's job and could handle it.

In and near the Vatican you see nuns in street clothes or in the distinctive habits of their orders, walking in groups or singly, who look as if they are at home there, and some of them actually are. There are also plenty of laywomen. Most of them are on their way to St. Peter's for worship or sight-seeing. At the entrance doors under the portico, men of the Vatican's Vigilance Service look visitors over. They would bar a woman with a plunging neckline, a bare midriff, or hot pants. (A conservative Spanish government minister remarked to me that priests had a *complejo del muslo* [thigh complex].) The Vatican dress code has nevertheless been relaxed for some time; pantsuits, once frowned upon, are okay now. People who are turned back (including men in flimsy athletic shirts) may rent a light raincoat-like garment to cover up excessive skin areas from entrepreneurs who often lurk nearby under Bernini's colonnades.

Among the females populating the papal state, especially on weekdays, are also participants in a once-in-a-lifetime audience the pope (sometimes wearing a black mantilla for the occasion and the requisite photo op); houswives who shop at the Vatican supermarket every few days; sight-seers touring the pontifical museums or the pope's luxuriant gardens; and laywomen with jobs in the Vatican or with relatives working there.

A Multifaceted Reality

The term *Vatican* covers several different, though related, things. First of all, the Vatican is a Roman neighborhood near the right bank of the Tiber River. It was slightly disreputable 2,500 years ago when Etruscan professional soothsayers dwell-

ing here issued *vaticinia* (prophecies) for a fee. Emperor Nero
(A.D. 37–68) built a circus at the foot of the modest hill; the
Apostle Peter, according to tradition, was buried there after
suffering martyrdom by head-down crucifixion.

Today the Vatican is a cluster of edifices with more than
ten thousand rooms, frescoed halls, staircases, and corridors
dating variously from the Middle Ages to the late twentieth
century. Some new construction or renovation work is in all
likelihood going on somewhere in the complex even as you
read these lines; the popes have always kept architects and
masons busy.

The Vatican's structures include the majestic Basilica of St.
Peter, the largest church in Christendom, erected in the sixteenth century to replace a fourth-century basilica built by Emperor Constantine over the presumed burial place of the Prince
of the Apostles. Adjoining it are the Apostolic Palace, where
the pope and his chief aides live and work; more than a dozen
small churches and chapels; and several other conspicuous
buildings housing world-famous museums, a two-million-
volume library, and offices. There are furthermore the barracks
of the Pontifical Swiss Guard and the papal security services;
a supermarket; a pharmacy; a residential hotel; an eight
thousand-seat modern audience hall; an oil-fueled power plant;
sober apartment buildings for employees; and—at either end of
the sloping Vatican Gardens—a railroad station and a heliport,
which is often used by the pope. Many of the women whom
you may see sweeping and dusting in the Vatican are personnel
of outside contractors.

Since 1929 the Vatican (or officially, the State of Vatican
City) has been the world's smallest sovereign entity. Its walled
surface, 108.7 acres, measures not quite seven times the area
of United Nations headquarters (which is not sovereign) on
Manhattan's East Side. Nearly two-thirds of the papal territory

is taken up by the Vatican Gardens. The tiny state has several detached appendages—buildings and other properties—in various parts of Rome and in the city's surroundings.

Vatican is also shorthand for the central administrative apparatus of the Roman Catholic Church—the pontiff and the bureaucracy directed by him—the way *the White House* may mean the U.S. president and government.

Finally, the Vatican is a multinational society with its own peculiar culture—male-dominated but in subtle ways also influenced by its female denizens. Vatican City is by language and many customs unmistakably Italian, even more narrowly Roman, yet there is nevertheless a sense of separateness. It's somehow like Switzerland's canton Ticino: most people speak Italian, eat pasta and polenta, and drink wine and espresso, but you are aware all the time that you aren't in Italy.

Among other things, one rarely hears a loud word, uninhibited laughter, or angry shouts in the Vatican. The high-decibel din of Rome's full-blooded everyday life remains outside the Vatican's walls. Vatican City's lanes, streets, underpasses, and gardens are much cleaner than Rome's. There are no garlands of laundry to dry on balconies and in windows as in many Roman residential sections, and no graffiti on the house walls. Vatican folk interact with more formality than do ordinary Romans most of the time.

Some eight hundred people live permanently in Vatican City, among them a few families with children. Only half of the residents enjoy the pontifical state's citizenship and are entitled to Holy See passports. More than two thousand employees—clerics and laypeople of either sex—commute to the papal enclave from other sections of Rome or places nearby every working day.

Seeming inconsistencies among the data on the Vatican population supplied here and in other parts of this book are due to the complexity of its elements: not all papal dignitaries and employees, including women, work in Vatican City; some who do are legally dependents either of the Vatican state or the Roman Curia or some affiliated agency; and others are housekeepers or relatives of residents.

Supermarket Faithful

Although there is no formal or informal female grouping in the Vatican, one place where its women can, and do, meet every working day is the Annona. This is a well-stocked modern supermarket for the papal state's residents, employees, dependents, and certain privileged customers—an emporium of food and household supplies that has long been something like a social center and, inevitably, an exchange for whispered inside news and rumors. Most of its customers are women.

Almost anything in the Vatican has a history of hundreds of years or longer. The Latin word *annona* goes back far more than two millennia: in ancient Rome it denoted the yearly supply of corn and its price to the end consumer; eventually the term came to mean provisions in general.

Like monasteries and other church institutions, the pope's own establishment has always been supplied in part with produce from its own landed properties and has often traded surpluses for other goods. When the State of Vatican City was created in 1929, its citizens and residents quickly found that they were saving money by shopping inside the small territory because it was exempt from Italian taxes and levied minimal or no import duties on items brought in from outside.

To be able to shop in the Annona is still a coveted privilege in Rome. Many local families resort to connections and ploys to gain access to the Annona by getting to use the precious *tessera* (Vatican pass) or winning the complicity of someone who rightfully holds it. Grandchildren of a papal physician, cousins of a long-defunct cardinal, nieces of monsignors—all would be regular Annona customers for themselves and friends.

The Italian government wasn't happy about Vatican-abetted tax dodging but didn't say anything publicly. Eventually under Pope Paul VI his deputy secretary of state, Monsignor (later Cardinal) Giovanni Benelli, ruthlessly pruned the shopping passes in circulation, ignoring the pained outcries from people whose *tessera* had been pulled. Nevertheless, today an estimated five thousand such credentials are still valid and in use. Diplomats accredited at the Holy See, convents, church colleges, and other institutions around town that are connected with the Vatican have them.

Today, after recent refurbishing, the Annona looks like a medium-sized American supermarket. Aisle after aisle under fluorescent lights is lined with broad shelves loaded not only with food but also with beverages, tobacco products, household appliances, toiletries, and some over-the-counter drugs. Tampons can be bought here; contraceptives can't.

Little loud talk but a lot of murmuring is heard at the Annona. A couple of nuns stack their shopping cart with containers of yogurt and juices, diffidently examining every single item. They are smilingly greeted by another brace of religious sisters who are also foraging for their convent. The four—two in black habits with white coifs, the other pair in brown garb and black caps—chat awhile in low voices.

Nearby a gray-haired woman in a modestly elegant suit looks at the labels of sparkling wines. "You like champagne, Miss?" asks a burly man, maybe an engineer of the Vatican's power plant or waterworks; they know each other. It's a joke, of course, and she explains with a giggle: "His Excellency has guests at dinner tomorrow." She is the housekeeper of a bishop or archbishop, evidently, and the man may have fixed a short circuit or a leaking faucet in their apartment.

More chatting can be heard at the checkout counter, although there is a quick line for up to nine items. Customers pay in cash or by credit card and get white plastic shopping bags without any signs on them; the Annona needs no publicity. From shortly after eight A.M. until afternoon, Monday to Saturday, a steady trickle of women and a few men carrying plain white bags walk out of the Gate of St. Anne; many have cars parked in the neighborhood. It's at the Annona and around it that a good deal of Vatican gossip originates.

The last time I visited the Annona, on a Saturday, I was brought in by a Vatican employee on her pass. The loudspeaker system inside announced that purchases could be made only in cash that day because of malfunctions by the ATM and credit card scanners. When we left the supermarket, we met a bespectacled nun who was wearing a gray raincoat over her blue garb, strands of gray hair sticking out from under her coif.

She was Sister Judith Zoebelein, an American member of the Franciscan Sisters of the Eucharist, and the Vatican's leading Internet expert. "They called me to the office, although APSA doesn't work today," she explained. "There is an emergency. All circuits have crashed, the computers are down." It was not yet nine A.M. The nun's acronym stands for the Latin name of the Administration of the Patrimony of the Apostolic See, the Curia's real estate branch. When the Vatican decided to start a website, its new Internet Office was incorporated into APSA. Sister Judith, as its director with the service rank of "technical assistant, first class," and her staff were assigned space in the Apostolic Palace. Whenever she was asked what training she had had for such a responsible job, she would say, none in particular, she just picked up the intricacies of Internet management as she went along. The official Vatican website is www.vatican.va.

Adjacent to the Annona is the Vatican Pharmacy, run by friars of the Hospitallers Order of St. John of God. The Romans call this group, founded in 1537 for assistance to sick people, the Fate Bene Fratelli (Do-Good Friars); the order also operates a hospital on Tiber Island, close to the Roman capitol.

Crowded with customers most of the time, the papal pharmacy dispenses prescription drugs, including some, imported from abroad, that are not or not yet licensed in Italy. You don't have to be connected with the Vatican to get access; just leave an ID at the booth of the Vigilance Service near the Gate of St. Anne and you get a temporary pass.

Many Romans and visitors from other parts of Italy, most of them women, buy Swiss, French, British, or American medicines in the Vatican or load up on over-the-counter health products or cosmetics, which are also available and attractively priced. Behind the long counters are white-coated friars and female pharmacists, all very knowledgeable and forthcoming with advice. The store hums with chat.

High-Level Buzz

Socializing on a different plane takes place at the new restaurant inside Vatican City. It is a part of the House of St. Martha, an establishment that could compete with a three- or even a four-star residential hotel. The modern building was erected at the cost of $20 million between 1992 and 1996 on the site of the old Hospice of St. Martha, close to the southern walls of Vatican City, off the left transept of St. Peter's. The 132 rooms and suites are to provide comfortable accommodations for the cardinals participating in future conclaves for choosing a new head of the church; meanwhile, they are used by prelates and distinguished visitors. Each guest must pledge to move out at once in case of a vacancy of the Holy See, to make rooms for a cardinal-elector.

During past conclaves the cardinals were cooped up in hastily prepared "cells" in the Apostolic Palace. Most of their accommodations were improvised, sparsely furnished, and prisonlike; the sanitary facilities were sketchy; and the entire election area was chilly in winter and stifling in summer. During the conclave of October 1978, which resulted in the election of Pope John Paul II, the participants and their attendants suffered greatly from the sweltering atmosphere because the outside temperature was unseasonably high and air-conditioning worked in only a small part of the premises. At the time is was suggested that the cardinals chose the Polish pontiff relatively quickly, on the second day, just to get out.

The Vatican guesthouse has an official Latin name: Domus Sanctae Marthae. It is managed by a nun of the Daughters of Divine Love and can be reached for reservations by fax. The restaurant for guests and visitors offers Italian food with few frills. A simple nun or laywoman of the papal administration wouldn't have a meal there unless asked by some dignitary. Pope John Paul II on various occasions has asked cardinals and other churchmen to lunch at the Domus Sanctae Marthae.

Many priests, monks, and nuns of the Vatican staff hurry to their colleges, communities, monasteries, and convents when their morning work is done, after one P.M., sometimes to return to their offices after lunch. Clerical and lay officials who live in Vatican buildings have their meals at home. Others dash out of Vatican City for a quick bite in one of the many trattorias and snack bars in the neighborhood, the old Borghi district, whose inhabitants and businesses have for centuries taken care of the material needs of papal personnel and pilgrims.

Other Vatican employees lunch on sandwiches at their desks.

The clerics of the Secretariat of State and other offices of the Curia used to have lunch in a special dining room, which has since been closed. The Vatican gardeners and other papal blue-collar workers have their own *mensa* (table), a cafeteria where they get wholesome, cut-price food. The one hundred or so Swiss Guardsmen use their own mess hall and tavern in their barracks. Off duty, they like to slip out in plainclothes to some pub or movie house. Local people are convinced that any blond Italian whose family has resided in the Borghi district was fathered by one of the pope's Switzers.

There is something like a coffee bar even in the big sacristy of St. Peter's, where canons of the basilica may have breakfast right after morning mass. When the Second Vatican Council opened in 1962, the bishops from all over the globe noticed that many of their Italian brethren would disappear for a while during morning and afternoon sessions in the Basilica of St. Peter. The foreigners soon found out that there was espresso and cappuccino to be had in a corner behind a side entrance, and gleefully adopted the Roman habit of an extended coffee break themselves.

The pontiff's statelet, after all, is still Rome, and the prevailing corporate habits are Roman. Between ten and eleven A.M., monks, priests, prelates, nuns, and lay employees of the Curia cluster around an espresso machine or a coffee dispenser (usually operated by a female colleague) to get their fix of caffeine and indulge in a little small talk and tame joking. Romans insist that because of their city's languorous climate, they just need a pickup, and non-Italian Vatican workers quickly convert to this and other local customs.

One place where churchmen and laypersons connected with the Vatican like to meet informally is at the opposite side of the Tiber, the Eau Vive (Living Water) restaurant. The name is an allusion to the well of Samaria where Jesus asked a Samaritan woman to give him to drink (John 4: 5–14). It's listed in Michelin's *Red Guide of Restaurants in Italy*, but it isn't just another trattoria. It is the flagship of a chain of similar establishments on all continents. They are operated by a community of laywomen, Travailleuses Missionnaires de l'Immaculée (Missionary Women Workers of the Immaculate Virgin), founded by the late Reverend Marcel Roussell-Galle in France in 1950. Together with groups of supporters, the organization was affiliated with the Carmelite order in 1987.

The Rome Eau Vive, in a sixteenth-century palazzo near the Pantheon, has two large dining rooms on the street floor, two sumptuous halls with vaulted and frescoed ceilings on the upper level, and a modern kitchen on the mezzanine. The staff is made up of young women (Eau Vive literature says "virgins"), most of them nonwhite. They wear the traditional dress of their tribe or native country if they serve at the tables, white smocks and low toques in the kitchen. They live together in a nearby building and during off-hours receive instruction in various subjects. They take temporary vows of chastity, poverty, and obedience but are not considered nuns.

The cuisine is mainly French, with a typical dish of some overseas country as the daily special. There is an ample wine list of French and Italian labels, some of them pricey.

The Eau Vive, a short bus or cab ride from the Vatican, has long been a favorite of the local gastronomic and social in-crowd, attracting residents and visitors who once in a while like to enjoy a good meal without the pasta dishes that are ubiquitous elsewhere in Rome. Among them are diplomats, priests, prelates, and Vatican personnel. When Pope John Paul II was still archbishop of Kraków, he would occasionally dine with friends at Eau Vive during his frequent sojourns in Rome.

Travel groups and individual guests are offered fixed-price menus in the downstairs rooms.

Eau Vive welcomes any visitor, and no perceptible attempt at proselytizing is made. Every evening at about nine P.M., however, the staff gathers around statues of the Madonna upstairs and downstairs to sing an "Ave Maria" while the lights are dimmed for a few minutes. Some patrons remain seated, others—especially priests and nuns—get up and join in the chant, then resume supper.

Vatican staffers meet with colleagues and officials of other branches of the Curia at Eau Vive, maybe cautiously exchanging views and experiences. Every now and then some nun working in the Vatican may be permitted by a superior at her office or the mother superior of her own order to accept a lunch invitation at that singular eating place, possibly together with a sister of the same community.

Information and gossip are also swapped between curial employees and other clerics in the refectories of various religious communities all over Rome. Yet I know of a monsignor belonging to the Vatican's Secretariat of State who lives and takes his meals in a college for postgraduate priests, strictly keeping to himself; he avoids contact with other residents beyond a friendly "good morning" or "good evening." Nuns of various communities have told me of similar aloofness by sisters with Vatican jobs. Papal employees in general are pledged to secrecy, but the staff of such sensitive departments as the Secretariat of State and the Congregation for the Doctrine of the Faith (once known as the Holy Inquisition) take special vows not to divulge anything they learn at work.

In such a climate of pervasive secretiveness, private parties of the kind described at the beginning of this chapter are essential for getting an idea of what's going on. Vatican clerics invite one another all the time and often ask nuns or even trusted laywomen to such lunches and dinners. No secrets are revealed, but through hints, jokes, winks, meaningful silences, and indirection, one may guess the drift of Vatican policies and obtain an inkling of the personalities and factions involved.

In past years I went for an hour or so once or twice a week to a semiprivate tearoom run by two middle-aged Englishwomen in a walk-up that a religious order permitted them to use. The place was near my office; the tea was excellent, there were also scones and cucumber sandwiches, and above all the company was good. Priests from the Vatican (even from the Secretariat of State), Jesuits from the Gregorian University, laymen, and a few women who had ecclesiastical connections were regulars. It was like an informal afternoon club where everybody knew everybody. I learned no secrets there but got a good feel for the unique atmosphere in clerical Rome and found that it is often flavored with a deadpan sense of humor. My favorite tea partners were a teaching nun and a Jesuit who both taught me how to read *L'Osservatore Romano*, the Vatican newspaper that comes out in the early afternoon of each working day.

"The *Osservatore*," the Jesuit told me, "seems as dull as *Pravda* and *Isvestia* under Brezhnev." (It still is today.) After a sip of tea, the Jesuit continued: "You have to read the *Osservatore* for what's not in it rather than for what is."

In much the same way, the diplomats accredited to the Holy See try to pick up inside information at the frequent embassy parties. There will always be a bunch of cardinals and archbishops present, maybe one or two laywomen with jobs in the papal administration, but hardly a nun, and any number of Romans of either sex who seem to have many (though often wrong) notions about Vatican affairs.

V

COMPUTERS AND CAPPUCCINO

The women who entered Vatican service as full-time employees during the second half of the twentieth century were at first typists, file clerks, secretaries, telephone operators, and translators. The mother superiors of some religious orders and other qualified nuns or laywomen were given advisory positions in Vatican agencies. More recently the female workforce in Vatican City and its appendages was augmented by archaeologists, art experts, sociologists, canon lawyers, communications specialists, and computer programmers. An American nun reached the rank of office chief at the Congregation for Institutes of Consecrated Life and Societies of Apostolic Life, the Curia's department for religious orders and kindred organizations; a laywoman was placed in charge of Vatican Radio's international relations.

The Vatican's women employees, like their male colleagues,

work for a plethora of interlocking, overlapping, and occasionally rivaling bureaucratic entities. Many, but not all, of these entities belong to the Roman Curia, which constitutes the executive and judiciary arms of ecclesiastical government. The administration of the State of Vatican City, which has its own civil and criminal judiciary branch and controls the pontifical museums, Vatican Radio, and some other papal bodies, is allied with the Curia but legally doesn't belong to it.

The word *curia* in ancient Rome first denoted a division of patricians, later the senate house. Since the Middle Ages the term *Roman Curia* has been applied to the machinery of papal governance. Today it is an organizational maze. Only to list its many sections and the names of its principal officials takes up 135 pages in the red-bound Vatican yearbook, *Annuario Pontificio*.

Some names recur several times: a cardinal may be the chief of a curial department and also sit on the directorates of three or four others; a titular bishop or archbishop may be the executive secretary of one division and a board member of two or three others. The administrative arm of the papacy is a self-perpetuating bureaucracy that through history has often conditioned the head of the church, especially when a pope was inexperienced, weak, timid, sick, or aged.

In its structure, the labyrinthine Curia resembles the architectural jumble of the Vatican buildings: there are corridors that seemingly lead nowhere, secret staircases, stuccoed and vaulted Renaissance halls, but also air-conditioned offices with fax machines and computers. The Curia spawns new committees and other bodies all the time. Through the centuries some papal offices have lost their power and most of their functions but keep bravely soldiering on while newer bureaucratic units accumulate influence.

A bishop from rich America or poor Zambia who comes to

the Vatican to seek a solution to some problem in his diocese or support in a controversy with the civil authorities back home feels lost in the tangle of sacred palaces and bureaucratic meanders unless he has an experienced mentor. The mother superior of a small congregation of nuns confided: "The heaven be thanked that a couple of our sisters are taking care of the household of [a senior cardinal of the Curia]. Through them I get His Eminence's advice on how to go about getting anything done in the Vatican."

The Curia has 1,700-plus employees, including some 300 women. (Approximately 1,300 priests, monks, and laymen and 100 women work in other Vatican services.) Foremost in the Curia is the Secretariat of State, the Vatican's power center, which has its seat in the same Apostolic Palace overlooking St. Peter's Square that also houses the pope's private quarters and personal office. The function of the Secretariat of State can be compared with the combined offices of the prime minister and foreign minister of a secular government.

The Secretariat of State has lately tightened its control of the other curial branches. Those bureaucratic satrapies have such names as congregations, administrations, prefectures, tribunals, secretariats, pontifical councils, pontifical commissions, committees, and offices. There are also an Apostolic Penitentiary and a Pontifical Chancellery.

Relatively few women work full-time in the Secretariat of State and the nine congregations, which may be likened to the chief departments or ministries of a lay government. Each of these bodies is headed by a cardinal and teems with archbishops, bishops, monsignors, and lesser clergy. In curial parlance, the congregations are also called dicasteries, an awkward Greek-derived word that you'll rarely encounter in the English lexicon.

Female employees are more numerous in the so-called New

Curia. This is a collection of bodies that were established in the wake of the Second Vatican Council in conformity with its purpose to attune the church to contemporaneous life. Among them are the Pontifical Councils for the Laity, for promoting Christian Unity, for the Family, for charities known as "Cor Unum" (One Heart), for Justice and Peace, for Pastoral Care of Migrants and Itinerant People, for Culture, and for Social Communications. A proportionally high number of women—nuns and members of the laity—have full- or part-time jobs at Vatican Radio.

The Curia is the visible aspect of the Holy See, the latter being a shadowy concept that causes much confusion. The Holy See is not the State of Vatican City, which was established only in 1929, but the semantic expression of the papacy's age-old claim to sovereignty, inviolability, and worldwide spiritual authority independent of any territory or secular power. If the pope were again in exile as his predecessors were in the thirteenth and fourteenth centuries (in Avignon, France), the Holy See would be where he is. International law has recognized this unique status of the papacy in such treaties as the Acts of the Congress of Vienna, 1814–15. Today the Vatican issues its passports under the heading "Holy See" and accredits its diplomatic envoys—apostolic nuncios and permanent observers at the United Nations and other international bodies—as representatives of the Holy See, not of the Vatican state.

To outsiders the Holy See may be indistinguishable from the State of Vatican City, but to legal sticklers they are separate. Papal rigorists wince when, for instance, the United States, which doesn't care for such subtleties, accredits its ambassadors to the Vatican state instead of to the Holy See. For day-to-day affairs, the civil administration of the State of Vatican City is under the orders of a lay governor who receives his instructions from a cardinals' commission.

Little Vaticans

The pope's official residence, the fifteenth-century Apostolic Palace, and the contiguous buildings enclosed by the Vatican walls have long since become too small for the proliferating pontifical bureaucracy despite their many rooms. Considerably more office and residential space was created when after a financial windfall produced by the Lateran Treaty of 1929 Pope Pius XI launched a vast building program inside and outside the new ministate.

The kingdom of Italy, then under the dictatorship of Benito Mussolini, turned over to the papacy a lump sum that at the time was worth $80 million to indemnify it for church property seized by unified Italy six decades earlier.

Pius XI, a practical-minded Milanese, decided that a part of the money received from the Fascist government should be used for the construction of a Governor's Palace behind St. Peter's as a visible symbol of Vatican statehood. Other new buildings, including a railroad station, also went up within the old walls ringing the newly sovereign territory. (Much of the spacious terminal is now used for nonrailroad purposes because the traffic on tracks linked with the Italian rail network has over the past several years shrunk to a few freight trains carrying merchandise for the Annona and other Vatican entities.)

The architects hired by Pius XI designed the post-1929 buildings in a style blending neo-Renaissance elements with the Mussolini Modern school of pseudoclassical grandeur then fancied in Italy. The resulting structures look frigid, if not frowning; they have severe porticoes, huge staircases, long corridors with many tall doors to individual offices, travertine floors, and twelve-foot ceilings. In the cold months the clerics who have apartments in those buildings and their female housekeepers (as well as the employees who work in the offices there) complain to the Vatican's real estate administration that the heating is inadequate—when the radiators, owing to some defect, haven't remained altogether cold.

In the papal building boom after 1929, several office and residential projects also were commissioned outside the Vatican walls, particularly at the approaches to St. Peter's Square. At the same time, the city of Rome, on orders from Il Duce, revamped a large part of the ancient, cramped Borghi district between the Tiber and the Vatican. Many old and decrepit houses were razed, and a new, broad avenue linking the river embankment with St. Peter's Square was laid out. The name, Via della Conciliazione (Reconciliation Street), was to remind future generations of the 1929 treaty that ended sixty years of conflict between the Italian state and the papacy.

The chief of the urban rehabilitation drive was Marcello Piacentini, a leader of the Mussolini Modern movement. It was his idea to line both sides of the new Via della Conciliazione with travertine obelisks topped by iron lanterns; the effect is that of a graveyard alley. The new buildings at either end of the avenue are Vatican properties. Their architecture, coordinated with Piacentini's blueprints, is less gloomy than that of the post-1929 structures inside the Vatican, also because their facades aren't a forbidding gray like that of the Governor's Palace, but honey-colored.

Today the buildings on the Via della Conciliazione and nearby, including a Palace of the Congregations, are occupied by curial offices and the headquarters of Vatican Radio. Several cardinals and other high prelates have their residences here. Some of these apartments on the top floors boast terraces and can be used (as many are) for cultivating little private gardens. The housekeeper of one fortunate tenant of such a suite confided: "His Eminence and I, we spend a lot of time puttering about our roof garden and we never tire of gazing at the marvelous panorama—St. Peter's Square and the facade and dome of St. Peter's. Whenever His Eminence has visitors from back home, he always takes them out to our terrace first thing." Cardinals are forever scheming to get one of those coveted apartments; small wonder there is a long waiting list.

Another huge complex of new edifices was built under Pius XI in the Trastevere district, on the right (northwest) bank of the Tiber like the Vatican but one and a half miles downstream. Trastevere was then in part a slum, inhabited by proletarians and lower-middle-class Romans proud of their own folklore and earthy dialect. Today the neighborhood with its many narrow, twisting lanes still has a slummy appearance, although it has long been gentrified, becoming trendy, cosmopolitan, and traffic-clogged. It is dotted with restaurants and taverns; Americans and other expatriates have moved into many of the tacky-looking walk-ups, outfitting their apartments with state-of-the-art kitchens and bathrooms. The poor artists and bohemians who once were denizens of Trastevere have been crowded out and moved to cheaper dwellings farther down the river.

The Vatican outpost in Trastevere was built as a sprawling annex of the medieval church and convent of St. Calixtus (pope from 217 to 222) and has become known as the Palace of St. Calixtus or, in Italian, San Calisto. It is a large, triangular complex of dark-gray five-story wings around a courtyard and parking lot. Ringed by an iron fence, the buildings look sullen on the outside, cheerless inside.

The Palace of St. Calixtus houses various offices of the New Curia with a considerable number of female employees and is the home of several cardinals and other clerical dignitaries. The high-ceilinged apartments on the top floors are much in demand for their sweeping terraces and superb panorama, which embraces the dome of St. Peter's; the Janiculum, Palatine, and

Capitol Hills; and Rome's historical core beyond the Tiber. "From each of my windows I have a different grand view," gloated a new occupant as he led a visitor through his eight-room suite. "On the terrace my predecessor grew wine, and so shall I."

The architects wasted a lot of space on imposing staircases and intimidating corridors in the palace. Legally a detached piece of the State of Vatican City, it has a blue mailbox of the papal post office in a doorway and a papal gasoline pump that dispenses fuel at rates that are considerably lower than those of the service stations a few hundred yards outside the iron gate. Many Vatican employees, nuns conspicuously among them, commute to their jobs by car and of course fill up at the papal pump, which is exempt from Italian taxes—a fringe benefit.

Another detached unit of the Curia is smack at the center of Rome, off the Spanish Square. It is the seventeenth-century Palace or the Congregation for the Evangelization of the Peoples, the Vatican's missionary arm. This branch of the papal administration was long officially known as the Congregation for the Propagation of the Faith (in Latin, *Congregatio de Propaganda Fide*). The modern term *propaganda* is derived from the old name of this Vatican body. Since *propaganda* has acquired a negative flavor and missionary activities suggest colonialism, the new title was meant to soothe the sensibilities of developing countries.

The department is nevertheless still in the business of seeking conversions to the Catholic faith in Africa and Asia besides administering the church institutions that are already there. The numerous missionary orders of women are important instruments in this field; their mother superiors and other members often visit the building, which the Romans keep calling "the Palace of the Propaganda."

Like the complex of St. Calixtus in the Trastevere district, the building off the Spanish Square is extraterritorial; Italian police are not permitted to enter it unless requested, and some Italian laws don't apply on its premises.

The Congregation for the Evangelization of the Peoples also owns properties in various other places and has a budget of its own, fed by contributions from the faithful all over the world. It runs a large, modern college for student priests from developing countries on the northern spur of the Janiculum Hill overlooking St. Peter's Square. Known as the Pontifical Urban University (after the early-seventeenth-century Pope Urban VIII, who founded it), the institution teaches Chinese and other non-European languages in addition to the normal theological curriculum. The cardinal heading the missionary department and its college as well as the nuns who take care of his household live in a panoramic two-story villa with a well-kept garden behind the campus.

Other extraterritorial church compounds that house sections of the Curia or other Vatican services are:

- The sixteenth-century Palace of the Holy Office, now called the Congregation for the Doctrine of the Faith, adjoining the State of Vatican City on its south side. This important curial department is the Vatican's watchdog of orthodoxy, once known and feared as the Holy Inquisition. It still investigates alleged heretics and schismatics. If found guilty, they can be excommunicated but are no longer burned at the stake. The building looks appropriately somber. Despite the supersecret atmosphere in its offices, its employees know that the pope's Secretariat of State is continually attempting to encroach on, and extend its control over, their department, but with little success so far.

• The Palace of the Chancellery, an enormous gray Renaissance building with a beautiful double-arcaded courtyard near a picturesque square, the Campo de' Fiori, where the priest-philosopher Giordano Bruno was burned alive for heresy in 1600. The Chancellery once handled weighty matters of papal governance, but it has long lost much of its old power. The palace today serves mainly as the seat of the Vatican's ecclesiastic tribunals. The best-known of them is the Roman Rota because one of its tasks is to issue ultimate sentences in cases of petitions for marriage annulment, which in Catholicism practically—though not doctrinally—substitutes for divorce.

• The Lateran, a group of buildings dating back to early Christianity, in Rome's southeast, comprises the Basilica of St. John, which is the pope's own cathedral in his capacity as bishop of Rome. The adjoining large palace is today the residence and office of the cardinal vicar of the city, who represents the pontiff in local ecclesiastical affairs. Many nuns and other female assistants are on his staff.

The pope's vicariate oversees 329 parishes, with 723 churches in Rome and its surroundings. Of the nearly eight thousand priests and more than twenty thousand nuns living in the area, only a fraction are available for pastoral work in the parishes, the others being employed in the Vatican, in educational institutions, or in other services. Despite—or maybe because of—such massive clerical presence, the cardinal vicar of Rome, Camillo Ruini, warned in 1994 that a large portion of Rome was "no longer Christian" and was in need of "re-evangelization." The city, and even some Catholics in it, was "subtly and pleasantly" invaded by a post-Christian mentality, the cardinal (a native of northern Italy) asserted: a stern denunciation of Roman dolce vita, which he reiterated many times later.

The Lateran complex also houses a university that trains students for the priesthood. It is considered a bastion of theological conservatism.

• The massive building of the Pontifical Gregorian University, erected in 1930 at the foot of the Quirinal Hill, is the church's principal institution of higher learning, founded by Saint Ignatius of Loyola in 1551 and to this day staffed by Jesuits. It is much more prestigious than the Lateran University; some of the lectures are in Latin. Today quite a few nuns and some laywomen attend classes side by side with students for the priesthood and postgraduate priests.

Why would a woman enroll in the Gregorian University even though she won't have a chance—at least not in the near future—to be ordained to the ministry? Antje, a Dutch student of the Gregoriana (she calls it "the Greg"), explained: "I want to hear Latin spoken as a living language and plan to teach it later at home. I have women colleagues at the Greg who take exams in canon law; many nuns go to classes because they want to become religion teachers or simply to have a solid theological grounding. Other women take social sciences."

Does she ever socialize with seminarians or postgraduate priests? Antje was asked. "Of course we talk and joke in the classrooms, often in Latin," she said, "and every now and then some of us will slip out for a quick cappuccino in the neighborhood. But they all return to their colleges and seminaries for lunch and they can't go out at night." The young blond Dutchwoman doesn't seem to have any trouble lining up nonecclesiastic dates in Rome.

• Yet another outlying appendage of the Vatican, also exempt from Italian jurisdiction, is the pontifical estate at Castel Gandolfo, 1,400 feet high in the hills sixteen miles southeast of Rome. The walled property, covering about a hundred acres, includes a stately villa from the seventeenth century; a modern audience hall for eight hundred people; a covered swimming pool that John Paul II had built at the beginning of his pontificate (to the astonishment of Vatican dignitaries); auxiliary buildings; an astronomical observatory staffed by Jesuit scientists; a park; and a small model farm. The farm grows vegetables for the pope's table and furnishes dairy products for his household and for the Annona.

The Castel Gandolfo estate is usually described as the pontifical summer residence, and its relative altitude and airiness indeed provide relief during torrid spells of the Roman summer. However, John Paul II has often spent time at Castel Gandolfo in the cool months, too, taking some of the Polish nuns of his entourage with him to the hillside. The permanent residents of Castel Gandolfo include the wives of gardeners and female members of the maintenance personnel.

• A vast transmission center of Vatican Radio with a cluster of towering antennae north of Rome is also an extraterritorial papal possession.

The Castel Gandolfo estate and the broadcasting center are administered by the government of the State of Vatican City, which handles the mundane matters of pontifical institutions. It is directed by a cardinals' commission and a lay governor; its more than thirteen hundred employees include many laymen and -women. The personnel enjoy the same benefits and have to observe the same rules as Curia staff.

Byzantinism and Legalism

Like any big bureaucracy, the Vatican has its own particular operating style, only more so. Precedents, which are often invoked, go back to the Middle Ages; files are known as "positions." The atmosphere in papal offices may overwhelm a new woman employee who isn't a nun. She will have to get used to unctuous behavior of superiors and some colleagues. The unspoken assumption is that the pope is inspired in his decisions by the Holy Spirit and that, to a degree, such divine guidance rubs off on his aides, the cardinals, archbishops, and bishops of the Curia.

A daunting legal edifice shelters Vatican and ecclesiastical business: the Code of Canon Law, last revised in 1983, enshrines the church's constitution and procedural rules in 1,752 Latin sections (canons). Papal legislation continually adds to that body of juridical norms. In its legalism the Roman Catholic Church is a true heir to ancient Rome and Byzantium.

Most Vatican offices seem dispirited to the outsider, also because of the solemn architecture and glum ambience. A visitor who by phone has obtained an appointment is shown by a doorman into a tidy waiting room with a few uncomfortable chairs, old pamphlets with some papal allocution on a table, paintings of saints or the Madonna by an obscure artist on the walls. The prelate or official whom the caller is to see shows up after a few minutes, and there isn't much, if any, small talk. One hardly ever has a chance to penetrate a papal office further than the waiting room.

The working language of the Vatican isn't Latin but Italian, even though one-third of the office personnel now aren't Italians. Subalterns—doormen, drivers, messengers, and maintenance workers—and the security officers are overwhelmingly Italian; the accent of most of them betrays their local Roman origins. Many are the sons, daughters, and other relatives of former or still serving Vatican employees; there are entire dynasties of papal dependents whose members at times show a proprietary attitude toward the Vatican. The Swiss Guards are native German- or French-speakers but generally pick up Italian and the local dialect quickly.

Many Italian—specifically, Roman—customs are softening the human climate in papal offices once you get accepted. The midmorning cappuccino break, when employees desert their computers and desks, is one example. Little gets done after the lunch hour: the siesta has been sacred in Rome since antiquity. Later in the afternoon work may be resumed in some departments, and may even go on until late if deadlines are to be met, but most of the women employees will already be off. Vatican dependents regularly work thirty-three hours in some departments, thirty-six hours in others, five or six days a week.

At work all members of the priestly staff address one another as "Father," "Monsignor," "Excellency," or "Eminence" even if they have to do so twenty times a day. Nuns are called "Sister" or "Reverend Mother"; laywomen, "Signorina" (Miss) or "Signora" (Mrs.) even though they may be on a first-name basis among themselves. A woman employee with a college degree is addressed as "Dottoressa" (Doctor) even if she holds just a B.A. or M.A. English-speaking clerics of the same rank may call one another "Bob" or "Jack" as they used to in seminary, but such familiarity during office hours isn't encouraged in the Vatican: Byzantine formality and obsession with titles is the norm.

The increasing number of personnel from central and northern Europe and from America since the mid-twentieth century has led to a relaxation of the clerical dress code. Priestly officials who are in the pope's immediate entourage or may be called into his presence still wear what he wants to see—a long black cassock or their order's garb. Nevertheless, in most papal offices many clerics don just a Roman collar and a dark suit—the costume that Italians, using an English term, call *clergyman.*

Nuns often come to work in a conservatively cut dark suit with a cross in their lapel or hanging from their neck rather than in their order's historic habits. A Roman woman in her late thirties who for several years has been doing bookkeeping work in a Vatican department said: "Of course, I wouldn't wear a pantsuit or blue jeans on the job. When I was younger, a miniskirt at the office was out of the question. My hems are well below the knee, and the necklines are always high. Nobody tells you in so many words to dress like that, but you get it pretty fast, and you want to keep your job."

Aside from the unofficial but well-observed dress code for women, the work climate in Vatican offices, once you know what you can and cannot do isn't dreary. "My boss, who is a monsignor from the north [of Italy], often cracks a mild joke," the accountant reported, "and you dutifully laugh, but not too hard and not too long. He roots for Juventus [a Turin soccer team], and I may make a facetious remark about the soccer championship and the frustrating Juventus performance. You wouldn't joke about his boss, who is an archbishop, or about the boss's boss, who is a cardinal, or heaven forbid, about the pope."

What about private use of the office phone? In Rome, secretaries and other employees appear to consider it their good right to make any number of personal calls during working hours. "Oh, I call my mother on my own cell phone whenever I have to work overtime," the accountant said, "and I'm careful about making personal calls on the office phone. Probably nobody would say anything as long as I didn't overdo it and got my work done, but we all know that all phones are bugged by the Vigilance [the Vatican security service]. My monsignor and the archbishop know it, too, although they have never said so to us."

Nor will a priest openly discuss office politics with female staff members, but they cannot ignore that jockeying for position and privilege is widespread in the Vatican, much as it is in any vast organization. Women personnel are hardly competing in the diffuse careerism, aware as they are of their limited possibilities: they know from the start that they can't rise above modest levels—the purple ceiling.

A married woman with a university degree who for more than ten years has been commuting by train from a town near Rome to a medium-rank job in a Vatican agency every working day said: "I like working for the Holy See because we are off on many religious holidays, not only the Italian national holidays, and have an annual vacation of twenty-seven working days. But I feel I'm qualified for a better job. However, forget about asking for a promotion or more money. That's a sore point. I belong, of course, to the Association of Vatican Lay Employees, but it can hardly do anything for us. A few years ago there was some communication with our employers, now there is almost nothing of that kind. All doors seem to have been closed."

The association representing nonclerical Vatican workers originated in 1979 among the technical personnel of Vatican Radio, and has since been joined by most of the lay staff of the other branches of the Holy See. It's the closest thing to a Vatican labor union, and in the 1980s it obtained salary increases, shorter hours, and improved working conditions in negotiations with papal officials. There has never been a strike in the pontifical state, although a few times there were go-slow agitations, one silent workers' parade inside Vatican City, and threats of work stoppages.

The highest pay that any woman employee can get—and very few do—is about $1,500 a month, thirteen times a year (a thirteenth monthly salary is due as a Christmas bonus). From time to time there are small extras: for the twentieth anniversary of Pope John Paul II's election to the pontifical throne in 1998, all Vatican lay personnel received $500 across the board. At the death of a pontiff the Vatican lay staff are, in keeping with an old privilege, entitled to a special gratuity, usually a month's pay. The new pope is also expected to grant them a bonus if the Holy See's finances permit such largesse.

In addition to their regular pay, which is tax-exempt, Vatican employees enjoy such fringe benefits as free medical care, access to the Annona, reduced-price gas for their cars, and possibly low-rent or free apartments.

For collective or individual grievances arising from employment in the Vatican, since 1989 there has been a Labor Office of the Apostolic See. Currently its fourteen-member consultative council includes one woman, a leading official of Vatican Radio, as a representative of the lay staff. The office's conciliation and arbitration board consists of two prelates and four laymen, all lawyers.

If conciliation fails and the result of arbitration is deemed unsatisfactory, the employee may request a ruling by the Court of Appeal of the State of Vatican City. This tribunal, dominated by clerics, would not be expected to decide against the interests of the papacy. The Holy See's labor relations have remained essentially patriarchal, and its judiciary cannot be described as independent.

Professional skills in women are appreciated in the Vatican, but they won't usually get them far, either. A woman translator in her forties who was born and educated in Germany, has lived in Rome for twenty years, and held her Vatican job for twelve said: "I love the work and never raise a question about overtime whenever a text has to be completed quickly. After my immediate superior, a layman, went into retirement, I was pretty sure I'd be promoted to his position. I wasn't. Instead, another layman, a German whose Italian isn't very good, got the job. Maybe if I were a member of the Opus, as he is, or of the Focolare, they would have given it to me."

Translators handle the documents that are one of the Vatican's main products. Papal addresses and encyclicals, apostolic constitutions, apostolic letters, pontifical exhortations, instructions from the congregations and other branches of the Curia to the hierarchy worldwide or in specific regions pour forth in an unending flow. Bishops in the field and rank-and-file priests often complain about the deluge of verbiage from Rome.

Pope John Paul II would write some of these texts himself in Polish, usually on the basis of memorandums prepared by various curialists and consultants; his draft would then be translated into Italian and by the Vatican Latinists into the church's official language. The resulting versions would then be vetted by the Congregation for the Doctrine of the Faith for theological orthodoxy, and possibly submitted to other departments of the Curia for their comments before final editing, translation into French, English, German, Spanish, Portuguese, and Polish, and publication.

In addition to the Vatican's continual output of ponderous documents, there are also many letters to governments, diplomats, prelates, other personages, and ordinary people all over the world to draft, revise, and translate. Women employees are usually involved in that cumbersome process. They, like all Vatican staff, have to take solemn vows never to reveal to anyone what they learn in the line of duty. Some top-secret texts are taken care of only by the chiefs of the translation services. The German woman's superiors evidently thought that a male member of Opus Dei or Focolare would be more trustworthy than she.

God's Work?

Opus Dei (God's Work) is a reticent—many say "secretive"—organization that was founded in Madrid in 1928 by the Blessed José Maria Escrivá de Balaguer and is today active on all continents. Conservative in its theology while stressing modern management methods in its worldly pursuits, Opus Dei runs in Rome a private university, a college for student priests, and other educational institutions. It was powerful in Spain during the last years of the Franco regime and still wields influence in that nation's church, politics, and economy. In addition to a well-regarded university in Pamplona, Spain, Opus Dei maintains centers of higher education in the United States, Canada, Latin America, Britain, Germany, and other parts of the world.

Because of its alleged elitism and furtive proceedings, Opus Dei has been called a Catholic freemasonry and an "octopus Dei." The Jesuits who in their early history had to face criticism and distrust similar to what Opus Dei has to deal with today are unsympathetic to the organization. Popes John XXIII and Paul VI regarded it with circumspection. An archbishop who was later to become a cardinal once confided to me that he had to be careful on the phone because the women operators at his switchboard were Opus Dei members and might spy on him. When the late Cardinal Giovanni Benelli was archbishop of Florence, he told me that Opus Dei priests among his clergy had a "conspirational" ethos and obeyed primarily the chiefs of their movement rather than him, their direct superior.

Such conflicting loyalties of Opus Dei priests were straightened out by Pope John Paul II, a great supporter of the organization, in 1982 when he granted it the status of a "personal prelacy" with worldwide ecclesiastical jurisdiction over its clerical and lay members. Escrivá, who had moved his headquarters from Madrid to Rome, died in 1975 and is buried in a marble tomb with the laconic inscription EL PADRE (The Father) in the stately Opus Dei building in the posh Parioli section, distant from the Vatican.

His successors, all Spaniards, have had since 1982 the powers and privileges of a bishop. Escrivá was beatified in a solemn ceremony in St. Peter's Square in 1992, a decisive step toward the proclamation of his sainthood, scheduled for October 2002.

The Vatican statistical office gave the membership of Opus Dei in 1999 as 1,780 priests, 344 seminarians, and 81,954 laypeople. There was no indication as to how many women were members. At Opus Dei headquarters in Rome and at the movement's residences, where many members live together in small communities, men and women are rigorously separated, although female members do housework for the men during the day. Some Opus Dei women also reputedly take care of the domestic establishments of Vatican prelates, although the latter seem to prefer housekeepers belonging to an order of nuns or to Focolare.

Opus Dei is wealthy thanks to the contributions it receives from rich or well-earning members and loosely affiliated benefactors. Earlier ascetic practices recommended by the Blessed Escrivá, like self-flagellation by male or female adherents, have been glossed over lately in Opus Dei drills, but some zealous members are known to continue sleeping periodically on the hard floor and inflicting on themselves other forms of penitence. Most of such information comes from former Opus Dei men and women who have left the organization; because of the resentment that usually marks such defections, it must be viewed with caution.

Under Pope John Paul II the prestige of Opus Dei rose owing to the accomplished professional performance of his official spokesman, Joaquin Navarro-Valls, a Spanish journalist, nonpracticing psychiatrist, and high-ranking member of the organization. Dr. Navarro was able to speak with authority on papal affairs because he had daily access to the pontiff, was often a guest at his table, and accompanied him on his frequent travels. The spokesman's small Vatican press office staff included male and female Opus Dei members.

Catholic Hearth

Focolare (Hearth) is a movement of predominately female lay-people (who call themselves Focolarini), but there are also male lay members as well as a number of priests and a few bishops. It was founded at the end of World War II by Chiara Lubich, an Italian schoolteacher of Slovenian descent in her native city of Trent in the Alps. Miss Lubich, then twenty-three years old, gathered a group of young women in a basement, held with them gospel readings, and looked after the needy in poor neighborhoods of Trent, which in 1943 and 1944 was the frequent target of Allied air raids. Several members of the group began living together like nuns.

Focolare became a movement that spread throughout Italy. Local bishops approved of the network, and some clergy joined. The Vatican first took official notice of the group under Pope John XXIII, who encouraged it. Focolare won adherents in other European countries and eventually on other continents.

At the turn of the millennium, the movement, still led by the charismatic Lubich, claimed to be represented in 182 countries with more than 4 million members and sympathizers, almost half of them active. Focolare units operate social welfare programs and publish magazines.

Several Focolare groups consist of women who have taken vows of chastity and are living together while employed in various secular jobs. At universities and elsewhere they often seek "dialogues" with Christians outside the Church of Rome and members of other faiths, including Buddhists, Hindus, and Muslims.

Focolare has adopted poor villages in Mexico and other countries as its "Little Towns," founding and operating schools and providing other services there. In 1991 the movement branched out into economic thinking and practice by getting involved in, or starting, small companies, first in Brazil and then elsewhere.

The rhetoric of Focolare stresses "joy," "mutual love in the spirit of Jesus," and "universal solidarity"; it pledges its members to a "life of authenticity." What is an outsider to make of such high-minded intentions? The many members of the movement I've met in Rome and in the offices of papal diplomats in other capitals have all been markedly cheerful and polite.

Whenever I tried to learn more about the special culture of their movement, they didn't exactly clam up, as Opus Dei members would, but usually remarked that the way of life proposed by Focolare was difficult to explain and must be experienced: "Care to join?" I was often reminded of the old Latin epigram: "Iesuita est id quod nemo scit nisi Iesuita sit" (A Jesuit is something that nobody knows unless he be a Jesuit).

The Vatican today regards Focolare as an "ecclesial movement" of the laity like some three dozen other groups, such as Communion and Liberation in Italy, the Cursillos in Spanish-speaking countries, and the International Catholic Charismatic Renewal. Miss Lubich was given an official Vatican position as a consultant to the Curia's Pontifical Council for the Laity. Many prelates turn to her whenever they need personnel for their offices or their private establishments. Focolare is well represented among the female staff of Vatican Radio.

Relaxed Radio

The human climate at Vatican Radio seems less austere than in the departments of the Curia proper. Officially, the broadcasting arm of the papal government is defined as an "institution connected with the Holy See," and in church publications it is also often called "the pope's radio."

A small transmitter was inaugurated in 1931 by Pope Pius XI and Guglielmo Marconi, a pioneer of wireless telegraphy. It was housed in a little building in the highest part of the Vatican Gardens; in 1936 it moved into a much larger structure nearby that toward the end of the nineteenth century had been built adjacent to an old tower to serve as a summer residence for Pope Leo XIII and was later used by the Vatican Astronomical Observatory (which has since moved to Castel Gandolfo to get out of Rome's city lights).

Today Leo XIII's summer home is the technical headquarters of Vatican Radio, with some studios. The adjacent 550-year-old Tower of Nicholas V is now crowned with a tall antenna for FM transmissions and a radio bridge system linking headquarters with a thousand-acre transmission complex at Santa Maria di Galeria, ten miles northwest of Rome. That fenced-in property—under Vatican jurisdiction through a special accord between the Italian government and the Holy See—includes huge fixed and rotating antennae. Complaints about alleged pollution by electromagnetic fields (called *electrosmog* in Italy) caused by the Vatican antenna farm have been clamorously voiced by the population of nearby areas for years, and in 2001 negotiations between Italy and the Holy See aimed to curb any possible physiological damage to residents.

Vatican Radio transmits in forty languages around the clock and offers live coverage of papal journeys, often minute by minute. Since 1970 the system's programming and production center has been in one of the buildings just outside Vatican City that were erected during the 1930s.

The five-story structure on the Tiber embankment at the beginning of the Via della Conciliazione contains offices for the various language groups, some twenty studios, a big hall, a chapel dedicated to the Archangel Gabriel (who as God's messenger to the Virgin Mary is the heavenly patron of telecommunications), and a library.

Vatican Radio has proportionally more female employees than do the departments and agencies of the Curia. About 25 percent of the permanent staff of four hundred are laywomen, along with a few nuns. (It will be recalled that the female contingent of Vatican personnel is 10 percent.) Many of the scores of part-time workers who contribute to the production of Vatican Radio as linguists, researchers, script writers, or speakers are female. The atmosphere at Vatican Radio headquarters is often hectic but generally less gloomy than many other offices of the Holy See. Young women in pantsuits hurry through the long corridors, saying hello breezily and cheerfully to priests and laymen they pass; this is a busy place, and some live or recorded program is about to be broadcast at any time of the day and night.

Most of the male staff are laymen; only about fifty are priests or monks. No fewer than fifty-nine nationalities are represented among the personnel. Many of its women and some of the men belong to the Focolare movement or other groups of the Catholic laity.

From the beginning Vatican Radio has been in the hands of the Jesuit order, though under the supervision of the Curia, especially the Secretariat of State. The president, director general, program director, and technical director of "the Pope's Radio" are all Jesuits. More than a dozen other priests of the order have key posts. The closeness of Vatican Radio to the pontiff was reinforced under John Paul II when the president of the system, the Reverend Roberto Tucci, was entrusted with organizing and managing thet pope's frequent journeys. (Father Tucci became a cardinal in 2001.)

Running Vatican Radio day after day means occupying a formidable position of power within the church. The Jesuit order is also influential in other ecclesiastical sectors in Rome: Jesuits are instrumental in the operations of the Pontifical Gregorian University, the Pontifical Bible Institute, and the 430-year-old Astronomical Observatory at Castel Gandolfo, officially known by its Latin name, Specola Vaticana (Vatican Watchtower).

There were insistent rumors in clerical Rome during the 1980s that Opus Dei, the modern rivals of the Jesuits, would take over Vatican Radio to guarantee the absolute orthodoxy of its programs. The ambitious organization whose fundamentalist theology and businesslike efficiency were much appreciated by Pope John Paul II would doubtless have loved to extend its growing influence to the Vatican's broadcasting arm. Such a coup didn't seem totally unlikely, because of the strong liberal currents within the Jesuit order at the time.

Such tendencies had already been noted during the Second Vatican Council and became strong under the Jesuit order's general superior from 1965 to 1981, the Most Reverend Pedro Arrupe y Gondra (a Basque, like the order's founder, Saint Ignatius of Loyola).

In Latin America some Jesuits espoused the cause of revolutionary "liberation theology"; in the United States, the Netherlands, and other countries, members of the order spoke out against the church's official stand on birth control and for the admission of women to the priesthood. Popes Paul VI and John Paul II told Father Arrupe and his aides on various occasions that they were deeply worried about liberalizing, even left-wing, trends in the 450-year-old elite order.

The Society of Jesus weathered these storms and, under Father Arrupe's successor as its general superior from 1983, the Most Reverend Peter-Hans Kolvenbach, a Dutchman with extensive Middle Eastern experience, appear to be regaining Pope John Paul II's trust. The perceived Opus Dei maneuvers aimed at securing a foothold in Vatican Radio remain futile. The services that Vatican Radio's president, Father Tucci, rendered the pontiff during his trips may have been a factor in the subterranean power play.

The general tone of Vatican broadcasts nevertheless sounds noticeably more broadminded than that of other papal mouthpieces. "We are quite receptive to new ideas and attitudes," a woman editor of one of the language sections said. "We are much more open than, for instance, *L'Osservatore Romano*," the Vatican's daily newspaper, which is theologically and culturally archconservative.

Vatican Radio's programs include a kind of court bulletin detailing the day's activities of the pope with live excerpts from his addresses and quotations from papal or curial documents. Newscasts provide round-the-globe information that is not confined to church affairs. There are also interviews with priests, missionaries, bishops, lay scientists, and other personages of general interest. For instance, the archbishop of Durban, South Africa, who had just been nominated as a cardinal by John Paul II, and a woman interviewer whose voice sounded very young candidly discussed the AIDS epidemic in Africa. A canon law expert explained in another interview that popes may resign if such a decision is not made under duress. If *L'Osservatore Romano* had published such a statement, it would have been interpreted as a hint that John Paul II, then nearly eighty-one years old and frail, was about to step down. Coming from Vatican Radio, the comment caused little surprise.

Feature programs focus on church activities, the lives of saints, noteworthy buildings and customs, the experiences of pastors and missionaries, social problems, and historical reminiscences. One series of spoken essays in the English-language service of Vatican Radio ran under the curious title "Why I Remain Catholic Despite Everything." Music programs range from Gregorian chants to Bach and Mozart to jazz.

Vatican Radio is also distinguished by having a laywoman on its five-member directorate, one of the highest-ranking females in Vatican service. She is Solange de Maillardoz, member of a Fribourg, Switzerland, bankers' family that had rendered earlier services to the Holy See. Mrs. de Maillardoz is also one of the fourteen councillors of the Labor Office of the Apostolic See, representing the Vatican's lay employees.

In her Vatican Radio office, adjacent to that of the system's director general, she told me that she is in charge of the papal broadcasting station's international relations. "During the Holy Father's trips abroad and whenever there is some major event in the Vatican, networks in the United States and in many other parts of the world ask us for material," Mrs. de Maillardoz explained. The tall, unobtrusively elegant official said she has worked closely with the Vatican's Internet section and with its Television Center (which so far has no station of its own but produces or helps produce programs for networks in Italy and other countries).

Fees for the use of sound bites or major segments from programs are about the only income that Vatican Radio generates, since it spurns advertising. According to official data, the radio services cost the Vatican $20 million annually, an amount that will seem enviably low to secular network executives. A medium-level woman employee of Vatican Radio remarked: "Other departments of the Holy See always criticize us for weighing too heavily on the Vatican budget. We should really make some money ourselves by taking on publicity from selected clients." But so far, you won't hear Vatican Radio plugs for cars or baby food.

Muckraking

If the Vatican's women employees have little space for career maneuvers, they see plenty of them performed by their priestly colleagues and superiors. Quite a few of the female sources in this book told of the rivalry, ill concealed by clerical unction or smiling bonhomie, that they witnessed on the job: prelates would claim credit for work actually done by simple priests or nuns, secret denunciations were frequent, brazen flattery of superiors was common.

In 1999 a 297-page volume, *Via col Vento in Vaticano** (Gone with the Wind in the Vatican) denounced what it describes as a venomous human climate in the Roman Curia. "I Millenari" (the Millennarians) were indicated as the collective, anonymous authors. An editorial note at the beginning of the book explains that they were a group of clerics who were working or had worked in the papal administration. The lengthy exposé was brought out by a commercial left-wing publishing firm Kaos of Milan; it sold more than 100,000 copies after the

---

*I Millenari, *Via col Vento in Vaticano* (Milan: Kaos Edizioni, 1999).

Vatican gave it free and highly welcome publicity by opening an investigation to discover its author.

The ecclesiastical sleuths soon determined that Monsignor Luigi Marinelli, a retired Curia official, had been a major source. He had been serving in the Vatican for thirty-five years, reaching the rank of office chief at the Congregation for Oriental Churches, but never rose to the rank of bishop. After being found out he told reporters that he was just the spokesman for a group of clerics, Italians and non-Italians, who had collaborated on the book project. He and his friends had omitted from the volume "some of the worst episodes," Marinelli said.

The Vatican started disciplinary proceedings against Monsignor Marinelli at the Tribunal of the Roman Rota, which—among other legal business—deals with civil and penal cases assigned to it by the pope, on charges of calumny and disclosure of curial secrets. The name of Monsignor Marinelli disappeared from the 2000 edition of the pontifical yearbook (which ordinarily lists retired prelates). Marinelli died in Cerignola, in southern Italy, in October 2000. His family's request for a funeral in the local cathedral was turned down on a technicality: the edifice wasn't available because a wedding had been scheduled for that day.

Several passages in *Gone with the Wind in the Vatican* depict the bitterness of monsignors who have loyally worked in the Curia for decades but are not promoted before being sent into retirement; the personal feelings of the spokesman for the Millennarians are unmistakably delineated. The Vatican abounds with titular bishops and archbishops whose fictitious sees may be some town in North Africa or Asia Minor that boasted a cathedral and a flock of faithful in early Christian times but were eventually overrun by Muslims. "Curial bishops are just senior bureaucrats," the mother superior of a small congregation of nuns remarked to me. "We have much more respect for a real bishop in a real diocese who does real pastoral work."

Archbishops in curial service also get frustrated if they don't become cardinals in due course. *Gone with the Wind in the Vatican* narrates the case of a prelate who "bought" a cardinal's red hat by contributing $50 million to Solidarity, the Polish anticommunist labor movement that Pope John Paul II favored. The ambitious and, in the book, pseudonymous churchman—easily recognizable as Cardinal Fiorenzo Angelini—was said to be able to afford such generosity because he was in charge of Roman Catholic health services, which receive many donations. It also had helped, the volume notes, that the new cardinal was a friend and ally of a Christian Democratic politician (former Italian prime minister Giulio Andreotti).

Another prelate, according to *Gone with the Wind in the Vatican*, virtually blackmailed Pope Paul VI into raising him to the cardinalate by threatening to make Vatican secrets public. The book also dwells on alleged power ploys involving factions of Italian cardinals, not unlike the cabals by princes of the church during the Renaissance period.

The rancorous climate in the Vatican's bureaucracy was indirectly confirmed by Pope John Paul II in an address to pontifical officials in December 2000, two months after Monsignor Marinelli's death. "The Roman Curia must be a place pervaded by holiness," the pope admonished them in a speech replying to the formal Christmas wishes that the assembled prelates had extended to him. "It must be a place from which competition and careerism are thoroughly absent, in which the love for Christ prevails."

The thinly veiled rebuke, which appeared to corroborate the denunciations by the Millennarians, was believed to have been prompted by fierce maneuvering for advancement by curialists as John Paul II was drawing up a secret list of churchmen whom he intended to make cardinals. The names were eventually published in January 2001, and a consistory for the elevation of the new cardinals was held the following month.

In all the acrimonious muckraking of *Gone with the Wind in the Vatican*, the Holy See's women play a remarkably small role. The book hints that one Italian cardinal is a womanizer, but it doesn't say whether the females who are the objects of his advances are pontifical employees or outsiders. If there is sexual innuendo in the prose of the Millennarians, it alludes mostly to gay relationships, which would appear to be rampant in the Curia. One unidentified prelate is quoted as having jokingly remarked that he had taken a "vow of homosexuality" to avoid entanglements with women.

VI

CURIAL ROMANCES

Erotic tensions are likely to occur when men and women who are committed to permanent chastity share a work place with those who are not. Cautious flirting, clandestine and notorious liaisons, even outright scandals happen in the Vatican, as they do elsewhere; what's remarkable is that there are so few or, at least, that so little is heard about them. The church has always taught that human beings are generally prone to sin, and it has much experience in dealing with sinners.

Gone with the Wind in the Vatican tells of a young priest-diplomat at the apostolic nunciature in Bern, Switzerland, who fell in love, requited, with a nun on the staff there, and an affair developed. The priest had an influential patron in the Vatican and got a diplomatic job in another capital, and his ecclesiastical career remained unimpaired; the nun was transferred to a convent in a different place, a measure that probably hit her harder than her former lover felt his reassignment.

I myself know of a woman in her early thirties who was a relative of neighbors of mine in the Trionfale section of Rome; she was a Vatican employee and lived alone in a small apartment in a church-owned building. I saw her from time to time when she came visiting her cousin. Through her my neighbors occasionally got chocolates and cigarettes from the Annona. There are few secrets in a Roman condominium: my neighbors gave to understand that their cousin had a more-than-friendly relationship with her superior, a monsignor. For a number of years the woman spent her vacations in Switzerland in August just when the monsignor absented himself from the Vatican. Her relatives were convinced that the two were together. If so, I can't imagine that the monsignor's peers and superiors would have been unaware of the situation. Over the years I have heard three or four stories of clerics, presumably attached to the Vatican, meeting women more or less regularly in the latters' own homes or in rented pads. Romans usually have a tolerant smile for such hanky-panky.

The apartment of my neighbors' cousin was probably obtained through her monsignor. Rents for church-owned living space were traditionally below market rates, but recently the Administration of the Patrimony of the Apostolic See (APSA), which manages Vatican real estate, has adopted commercial standards in some (but not all) new rental contracts.

Many of these apartments in Rome are inhabited, usually still at relatively low rents, by clergymen, Vatican employees, and relatives of employees as well as by other people with good ecclesiastical connections. Such contacts are as a rule developed over years, if not generations, but sometimes they come about more quickly, particularly if there is a romantic interest.

Liaisons, Flings

A lively woman employee of a Curia-affiliated agency was asked point-blank: "Could you live with a man, maybe a former priest, without being married to him?" She isn't Italian and didn't seem shocked by the question. "One would have to be very, very discreet," she replied, "especially if one had an apartment that is owned by the Holy See outside Vatican City. Inside Vatican City it would be impossible; you'd be asked to get out and would be fired from your job. But cohabitation isn't necessary for a liaison, even a long or permanent one, is it?"

With a conspiratorial smile, she volunteered: "I know of one lady of a certain age in a Vatican position who has a very active social life. She comes from a family with a lot of money and must have got her present job through a prelate friend of her influential father. She lives in her own apartment and is running what I'd call a clerical salon. She asks friends and acquaintances from the Vatican and from outside to tea on weekends and even gives small dinner parties for them. I myself was her guest a couple of times; it's all very pleasant."

The neighbors in the partygiver's condominium, a short bus or cab ride from St. Peter's Square, know that she works for the Vatican, and sometimes they beg her to get them a bottle of scotch or the like from the Annona, our informant reported. The neighbors are used to seeing clerical types in the lobby or elevator; there is no prying *portiere* (resident janitor) in the building.

"I won't say my friend is having an affair with someone, maybe a priest, but she might as well," our source said archly. "On some weekends there may just be tea for two at her place."

Another woman, a college graduate and a native English-speaker as well as a linguist, came to Rome in the late 1990s for what was supposed to be a year's study of art history. On one of her first evenings in the city she went alone to the Quirinetta movie theater, which screens films in their original language, to see *Titanic*. She happened to sit next to a middle-aged man in dark street clothes. They started talking, and he told her that he was a priest. That same evening he said if she wanted a part-time job while in Rome, there was an opening at his Vatican-linked institution, which housed English-language students for the priesthood.

When I spoke to her months later, she was the secretary for a bishop and graphically described to me the atmosphere in the college that he directed: "Half of our students are gay; some of them have become good friends, and we go out for a pizza now and then. I leave the others alone, although one or another seemed in the mood of flirting. A priest [in the same institution], however, gave me a hard time. He offered to seek dispensation from his vows and give up the priesthood to marry me; he would earn a living by teaching or social work. I told him I had become engaged to an Italian in a solid professional position, was in love with him, and was going to be his wife. My ecclesiastical suitor cried and declared that he was heartbroken. He is still a priest and we avoid talking to each other."

Priests resign from the ministry all the time, often to live with women or go through a civil marriage ceremony. To marry in the church, as many ex-priests want, they have to petition the Vatican for release from their vows, which is a lengthy procedure called laicization. Since the middle of the twentieth century, it has been granted much more often than it once was.

Nevertheless, many members of the Curia were shocked when, late in 2001, the director general of the Vatican Television Center, Monsignor Ugo Moretto, formally requested to be released from the ministry because of his involvement with a woman. The forty-five-year-old tall and chubby monsignor from the Veneto region had been heading the papal video services for five years and had been in the entourage of Pope John Paul II during some of his journeys. He had expanded the Vatican's television presence during the 2000 Jubilee Year and had announced an ambitious Beyond 2000 project for the production of new programs. There was some head-shaking in the pontifical administration when he asked for additional funds to realize his plans.

In the late summer of 2001, Monsignor Moretto informed his bishop, the Most Reverend Antonio Mattiazzo, of Padua, that he intended to resign both from his Vatican post and from the priesthood. The bishop asked him to remain a member of his clergy and promised that he would find a challenging position in the Padua diocese for the monsignor.

However, Monsignor Moretto insisted on leaving the priesthood, because his companion of a few years, a thirty-two-year-old divorced journalist from Padua, had become pregnant. In November 2001 he formally petitioned the church for "reduction to a layman's status," explaining that he wanted to marry his companion in a religious ceremony. The ecclesiastical authorities suspended the monsignor from saying mass and performing other priestly functions; to become a layman in the eyes of the church would take many months.

The former head of the Vatican television arm explained in interviews that "my crisis arises from the difficulties to keep my roles as a priest and as a media manager apart." He went to live with his companion in a condominium in a Milan suburb and said he was looking for a job.

Some members of the Roman clergy seek fleeting adventures. Once in a while a naive or incautious cleric is rolled by a prostitute or victimized by a pimp. Rome police always handle such episodes with the utmost discretion, often in cooperation with the office of the pope's cardinal vicar for the city of Rome. Surely, no Roman official of whatever ideological persuasion would have disclosed so many details about the dismal case of a cardinal's death as were made public in Paris in 1974.

The churchman was Cardinal Jean Daniélou, a sixty-nine-year-old Jesuit theologian and writer, a friend of Pope Paul VI, and a member of the French Academy. He suffered a fatal heart attack in the building of a twenty-four-year-old woman, described as a nightclub stripper and call girl. The cardinal, who was wearing civilian clothes (as he often did), seems to have been shadowed by the police for some time, maybe for his own protection. A large amount of cash was found on his body, apparently destined for the young woman he was about to visit. French church officials explained that the cardinal had befriended the woman for some time, had helped her financially, and had attempted to induce her to mend her ways.

Many Romans will tell you that in olden times, apparently until the late eighteenth century, a brothel operated exclusively for clergymen in the city. Everybody seems to agree that it was located in the Via Giulia, the rectilinear, once distinguished street close to the left bank of the Tiber that Pope Julis II (1503–13) had built. I have never been able to verify the story, which may be an urban legend. It is at any rate characteristic of Roman leniency regarding sex and the clergy.

In the Renaissance era a religious society in Rome took care of the papal city's many prostitutes, seeking to have them change their way of life and, above all, ensuring that their children, then numerous, would get an education to enable them to lead an honest existence. Today a special committee of the standing group of the superiors of female religious orders deals with the plight of Eastern European sex slaves and voluntary prostitutes who since the collapse of the Soviet Union have invaded Rome as well as the rest of Italy and other European countries.

Rome's sexual temptations, to which celibates are susceptible in the same way or even more so than other people, have at all times been formidable. Today soft-core pornography is prominently displayed at all newsstands, even at those close to the Vatican; wall posters in streets and squares detail the anatomy of luscious women and handsome men; street prostitution and the call-girl industry count thousands of practitioners, some in their teens.

Every level of Roman society has always included women whom people in the know would characterize as "cassock-crazy"—lusting for priests. "What a waste," the wife of a counselor at an important embassy whispered to a friend at a diplomatic reception, indicating with her eyes a strapping young Polish monsignor from the Vatican. The meaning: shouldn't such a hunk be a player in Rome's erotic sweepstakes? Five minutes later the woman was no longer talking to her friend but had sidled up to the monsignor and apparently tried to persuade him to have another glass of champagne.

Priests working in the Vatican, especially in the Secretariat of State, have a way of looking more elegant and acting more polished than do ordinary clergy: their long cassocks are of fine material, their Roman hats are often worn at a rakish angle, they are carefully groomed, and they aren't embarrassed if women—and sometimes men—make overtures to them in casual encounters or at official parties.

In the Vatican offices it is highly unlikely that a female employee would flirt as openly with a priest, handsome though he may be, as the counselor's wife did at the embassy party. However, some of the Vatican's women have been known to start living with a man, maybe even a former member of the clergy, without being married to him. If such a female employee is found out (which doesn't necessarily happen), she is usually dismissed and has little chance of redress by the Holy See's labor-grievance mechanism.

Male lay employees of the Vatican may be flirtatious too, as Wanda learned. She is a Croatian student in her early twenties, a distant relative of the late Cardinal Franjo Seper, who was prefect of the powerful Congregation for the Doctrine of the Faith. She already spoke good Italian—in addition to German, English, and some French—before she came to Rome to earn a degree either in archaeology or art history. Through a monsignor who as a young cleric had been close to Cardinal Seper, she landed a part-time job as a receptionist–telephone operator at an office of the Curia near St. Peter's Square.

She quickly learned to field the international calls to the direct telephone number of her office, which bypassed the Vatican's central switchboard. Showing visitors into her office's waiting room, she would have some friendly words for each. Tall and blond, with a ready smile, Wanda soon was popular with the priestly staff, the nuns, and the laypeople working in her office.

If she was asked to do an errand or other small service for someone, she would do it reliably and well; with her sunny nature, she was a big success in the Curia. "You have done us a good turn by introducing Wanda," the cardinal who was the chief of the office is supposed to have told the monsignor who had originally brought her in.

One occasional visitor was a member of the Vigilance Corps of the State of Vatican City—let's call him Marco— thirty-nine years old (that's what he told her), good-looking with his dark hair and dark eyes, though a little overweight. He liked to linger at Wanda's desk in the corridor near the entrance and chat with her for a few minutes before having himself announced to the official he had to see.

Marco never told Wanda what business brought him to her office, but he did mention that he had done police work during his military service with the Italian Carabinieri before joining the Vatican security agency. "Through the centuries faithful," he would say, reciting the Carabinieri motto.

"Faithful to whom or what?" Wanda once asked. "I bet to yourself."

"To the Roma," Marco replied in mock seriousness, meaning the soccer club he supported.

After work one afternoon, Wanda ran into Marco outside her office. "May I offer you a cappuccino at that place around the corner?" he asked. She said she had drunk more coffee than was good for her at work, but if he wished, he could walk her to the nearby bookstore on the Via della Conciliazione, where she had to pick up a volume for a bishop in her office. With the book in a plastic bag, Wanda said she had to catch a bus to get to a lecture at the university that she couldn't miss. Saying good-bye, Marco held her hand a little longer than she would have expected. It was a Friday, and Wanda got to her lecture just in time.

On the afternoon of the following Tuesday, she again found Marco outside her office. She smilingly asked, "Am I under surveillance by the Vigilance?"

"Not by the corps but by me," he answered. That time she did have a cappuccino with Marco.

For a month they met a couple of times each week, and once went to the Giulio Cesare multiplex to see a movie. In the dark he held her hand and lightly kissed her on the cheek. Afterward they had pizza and some wine at a nearby café before Marco had to return to the Vatican. "Let's have dinner at some nice restaurant next time I'm off duty," he proposed. She didn't say yes or no.

Two days later, before noon, Wanda answered the phone at her office, heard a woman ask for her by name, and when she said she was speaking, the woman started to scream: "Bitch: Leave my husband alone, you whore! If I catch you being after him again, you'll get such a beating that you'll never forget it, Vatican slut that you are! Letting a stupid man spend his money on you when his kids need shoes!" Wanda said nothing, cradled the phone, and felt like throwing up. She went to the monsignor who was her immediate superior and asked to be allowed to go home because she didn't feel well.

"You are frightfully pale," the monsignor said. "Shouldn't I call a doctor or someone from the health department?" Wanda told him she just needed to lie down and would take a taxi to the convent where she lived. This was again on a Friday. Her office was also open on Saturdays, but she called in to say that she was still a little shaky because of an upset stomach and would be back at work Monday.

On Saturday afternoon the nuns called her to the telephone; it was Marco. "I am speaking from a pay phone," he said in what seemed an altered voice. "I am awfully sorry for what happened yesterday. She is like a fury, you have no idea of what I'm going through. She got an anonymous call from a man who told her things that never happened. He must have given her your name and the place where you work."

"I had no idea that you were married and have children," Wanda said coolly.

"Yeah, two girls, but the marriage is a disaster. Biggest mistake of my entire life, my mother says so, too. Since I met you, I have been dreaming we could one day go abroad, you and I."

"Yes, and live happily ever after, forever faithful, as the Carabinieri say. Go and buy your girls new shoes and don't call me ever again."

When Wanda went back to work Monday, a young man in a Vatican messenger's dark blue uniform had taken her place behind the desk in the corridor; he told her that the monsignor wanted to see her. The monsignor no longer addressed her as Wanda but as *Signorina* (Miss). Without his habitual smile, he announced: "His Eminence has decided to reorganize this office; therefore, your services are no longer required. We can't give you full severance pay because you were only a provisional part-time employee, but a smaller amount is waiting for you at the cashier's. Good-bye and good luck!"

Wanda didn't see Marco anymore. For some time she explained the sights of Rome to tourists as a freelance guide, and eventually found another part-time job with a travel agency. The foregoing is Wanda's story. Marco wouldn't provide his version. He is still with the Vigilance Corps.

Such Good Friends

If Vatican insiders and Romans in general talk smirkingly about priests who have affairs with women, and about female employees of the Holy See with known boyfriends, clerical or otherwise, a lot is also said about gay relationships involving clerics. One who clamorously brought up the matter was the late Roger Peyrefitte. In his book *Les Clefs de Saint-Pierre** (The Keys of St. Peter's) and subsequent magazine articles and interviews, the French author named names and even hinted that Pope Paul VI was attached to a male actor whose name Peyrefitte withheld, but could be guessed easily. *Gone with the Wind in the Vatican* also mentions much gossip about allegedly gay prelates of the Curia.

In Rome one hears much less about lesbian ties in the papal state, although they do exist. The friend of a young woman who was, and maybe still is, involved in one told me about it. I admit that for once it's a secondhand story; while I am con-

---

*Roger Peyrefitte, *Les Clefs de Saint-Pierre* (Paris: Flammarion, 1955).

vinced it did happen, I cannot guarantee the veracity of all details.

The young woman, a tall and pretty college graduate in Italian literature (a degree that is nearly worthless in the job market today), landed a secretarial position in the Vatican through her uncle, who had become the bishop of a major Italian diocese after having served in the Curia for several years.

Let's call the protagonist of this account Anna. The Vatican job rescued her from deep depression: she had a few months earlier broken up with her boyfriend of four years, a just-graduated engineer who hoped to emigrate to the United States or Canada and had announced to her that he didn't feel like committing himself to a joint future. Anna had long introduced her friend as her *fidanzato* (fiancé) to family and acquaintances. For several weeks she had been despondent ("suicidal," I was told). Her mother, alarmed by the young woman's misery, got on her brother-in-law, the bishop: "Something must be done about Anna." That's how the Vatican job materialized. (Anna's great-grandfather had worked in the Vatican's administrative services, and the bishop had many friends at the Holy See.)

Anna was assigned to the archives of an office that was in the throes of computerization. To show her where files could be found and to pull them out quickly whenever they were needed, a nun who had been working in the section for several years was put at her side. On the first day the slim, pale nun, in her late thirties, looked at the newcomer and said, "What beautiful green eyes you've got." Then she started explaining what Anna's tasks would be.

At about eleven A.M. the nun produced coffee from a big thermos that made the rounds of the office and asked Anna questions about her studies and her family. A monsignor wandered into the archive room to ask if there was any more coffee left, and Anna was introduced to him. "We are really like a family here," the monsignor genially remarked.

"He's our boss," the nun whispered when he was gone.

After a few days Anna got the hang of what a filing clerk had to do and started familiarizing herself with the new electronic retrieval system. The nun who was her mentor kept dropping in with the thermos at midmorning and often lingered, saying little and gazing intently at Anna's face. After about a week, when the two women were alone in the archive room, the nun softly asked: "Why is a beautiful girl like you always so sad?" Anna mumbled something about personal misadventures of a sentimental nature and tried a brave smile that became sobs. The nun came close and stroked her hair, embraced Anna and kissed her on her cheek, got even paler than usual, and quickly left.

Over the next couple of weeks the nun got out of Anna most of her story about the ex-fiancé, and often kissed her. Once she confided: "I too suffered a lot last year when Mother Superior suddenly had a sister whom I loved transferred to another house of our order." Anna, who wasn't naive, didn't immediately grasp what the nun meant. She told her friend (a former classmate who much later became our informant) that she really felt soothed and was rather looking forward to the pale nun's consoling words and hugs.

The nun had become the secretary of the monsignor who had dropped in at the archive room on Anna's first day; she nevertheless kept visiting almost every day and stayed to chat a little whenever she was alone with Anna. If another staffer came in, the nun made a show of counseling Anna about the computer system, although she no longer needed such advice. By then she seems to have considered the nun one of her closest friends.

One Friday afternoon about a month after Anna had joined the office, the nun came to see her while she was watching the monitor, looked over her shoulder, and after a few seconds stepped to her side, taking the young woman's right hand from the keyboard, putting it on her own left side, and whispering breathlessly, "Feel how my heart is pounding!" Then she kissed Anna on the mouth, and quickly left. Anna later told her friend that only then did she realize what was going on.

"The nun must have been wearing something like armor under her habit," Anna was quoted as having reported. "A corset or a stiff starched undershirt. But I did actually feel her heart thumping. I wasn't really upset and maybe would have kissed her back if she had stayed, although I've never kissed a woman like that. I felt a little agitated myself."

Later Anna's confidences to her former classmate became sporadic. Asked about the pale nun, Anna would say, "Oh, I see her of course during coffee breaks, but there's nothing between us. I kind of feel sorry for her. I shouldn't talk about what's going on at the office. They made me swear never to speak to anyone except my superiors and colleagues about office matters."

The following summer the nun received permission from her order and from the monsignor whose secretary she was to visit her family in a hillside village north of Bergamo, in northern Italy, for two weeks. Her superiors thought she needed a little rest and country air. A few days later Anna, too, went on vacation, her first since she had joined Vatican service. Her former classmate said she was convinced, but had no positive proof, that Anna had followed "her nun," maybe to stay with her family.

Prelates in Love

A seventy-year-old retired archbishop who, after holding a position in the Roman Curia, got married in a televised ceremony
in New York caused no little discomfiture in the Vatican. The
main character in the bizarre affair was the Most Reverend
Emmanuel Milingo, born Lot Anthony Emmanuel Milingo
Chilimbu, whom Pope Paul VI in 1969 had named head of the
archdiocese of Lusaka, Zambia.

As the highest Roman Catholic prelate in the African
country, the archbishop soon caused bafflement at the Holy
See. The apostolic nunciature in Lusaka and other observers
worriedly reported that he had introduced unauthorized tribal
rites into the liturgy of the mass and the sacraments and that
he was practicing the exorcism of demons and forms of faith
healing. By 1983 Pope John Paul II, yielding to urgent rec-
ommendations from cardinals of the Curia, called Archbishop
Milingo to Rome to get him out of Africa. He was named a
special delegate in the Pontifical Council for Pastoral Care of
Migrants and Itinerant People and got an office in the Palace
of St. Calixtus as well as an apartment in a Vatican-owned
building opposite the Gate of St. Anne.

The black archbishop's curial job was ill defined and gave
him little to do. He used it as a base for building up a personal
constituency. He soon had a reputation as an exorcist and successful healer in Rome and eventually other parts of Italy.
Wherever he said mass, he made a joyous happening of it,
singing African songs, doing dance steps, and encouraging the
congregation to do likewise.

Quite a few people affirmed that he had cured them of
various illnesses. The strapping, charismatic prelate gathered a
following of thousands. I once saw his desk in his personal
office at the Palace of St. Calixtus: it was covered with scores

of letters and telephone messages asking him for appearances or individual treatment. His living quarters were often beleaguered by help-seekers, especially women.

The Vatican followed the African archbishop's activities with deepening concern. The cardinal archbishop of Milan and other members of the Italian hierarchy asked him to stay away from their dioceses, but he was still welcome in other parts of the nation. His songs on compact discs were widely marketed, and the archbishop became a media personality, making appearances in a white cassock with purple trimmings and a golden episcopal cross at the annual San Remo song festival and other shows.

By that time, conservatives in the Curia had decided that enough was enough, and had the archbishop deprived of his job at the Council for Pastoral Care of Migrants and Itinerant People and of his apartment close to the Vatican. He moved to Zagarolo, a town fifteen miles east of Rome, accepting the hospitality of a business owner whose daughter he had successfully treated. Milingo's curial enemies told one another piquant anecdotes about his healing practices.

The archbishop also founded a congregation of religious women, mostly Africans, the Daughters of the Redeemer, and was scheduled to conduct a three-day spiritual retreat for them in a convent near his new residence in early June 2001. Instead, he disappeared; he surfaced in New York a few days later.

On May 27, 2001, Milingo and a forty-three-year-old Korean acupuncturist, Sung Ryae Soon, were pronounced man and wife by the Reverend Sun Myung Moon. Fifty-nine other couples were simultaneously united in matrimony by Reverend Moon, head of the Unification Church, in a collective ceremony in the Trianon Ballroom of the New York Hilton Hotel. The archbishop wore a black dinner jacket with a white tie and white gloves; his bride was in a belled white wedding dress and a veil.

Milingo told reporters that the Reverend Moon had introduced him to a number of women candidates for marriage only a few days before the wedding rite and that he had chosen Miss Sung, whom he called Maria as a pet name, because he had liked her at once.

When he was asked whether he expected offspring, the archbishop chuckled and remarked: "If Abraham managed it at a hundred years of age, I may have some hope at seventy-one." His seventy-first birthday was just two weeks away.

The archbishop declared that he wasn't repudiating the Roman Catholic faith but expected that his relationship with the church would change. He had made his decision to get married, he said, advised only by Reverend and Mrs. Moon. He complained that the Vatican had "torn" him from Africa and charged that "they were afraid that I was getting too popular; they ridiculed me as a witch doctor. What I did, I did against Satan."

In the Vatican the first reports about the archbishop's defection were received with incredulity mixed with consternation. "Let's hope it isn't true," the pope's spokesman, Dr. Navarro-Valls said. The Vatican sought to contact Milingo through the Roman Catholic Archdiocese of New York but couldn't reach him. When television and newspaper reports presented evidence that Milingo had actually taken part in a marriage ceremony staged by what Italian media called the "Moon sect," Dr. Navarro declared that he had placed himself "outside the church." The spokesman expressed hope that the errant archbishop's many followers would "remain within the church," avoiding a schism.

While the African prelate and his new wife were visiting her family in South Korea, the Vatican's Congregation for the

Doctrine of the Faith issued a public ultimatum to Milingo: he had until August 2001 to declare his "faithfulness to the rule of celibacy" and obedience to the supreme pontiff to avoid excommunication.

In early August 2001 Milingo turned up in Rome by way of New York and Milan; was met by "old friends," including an Italian woman painter; and went with them to the papal summer residence at Castel Gandolfo. Pope John Paul II received him after a little while, although no audience for him had been scheduled officially, and the two had a long talk.

Afterward the Vatican stated that the pope had received "His Excellency Monsignor Milingo, Archbishop Emeritus of Lusaka," and that the audience was "the beginning of a dialogue that, it is hoped, could lead to a positive development." Implicit was that the deadline for excommunication had been lifted. Milingo told reporters in a press conference that the pope had been most kind to him but that he himself could not make any decision before speaking "to my wife, Maria."

Mrs. Sung arrived in Rome from New York two days later but was unable to contact, let alone see, "my husband, the archbishop." Milingo, it was learned, had started a period of prayer and meditation at a secret place, maybe a convent.

For television and the tabloid press, the affair of the good-looking, if chubby, Korean woman who was tearfully searching for a vanished prelate-husband was a godsend: a maudlin and melodramatic relief in a vacation period filled with grim news from the Middle East and the Balkans. The excitable Italian newspapers called the archbishop's bride "Lady Milingo," and reporters camped out in the lobby of the hotel near the Tiber where she was staying.

Mrs. Sung was quickly joined there by officials and followers of Reverend Moon's Family Federation for World Peace and Unification, who had arrived from the United States to lend support. Talking to the press, Mrs. Sung voiced the suspicion that the Vatican had kidnapped, maybe drugged, her husband to prevent him from meeting with her. She announced that she was going on a hunger strike, determined to die unless she could see the archbishop.

The Vatican issued photostats of what it purported to be a handwritten letter from the archbishop to the pope whereby he recommitted his life to the Roman Catholic Church, renounced his "cohabitation with Maria Sung," and announced that he had ended his relationship with Reverend Moon. The letter concluded with a pledge of obedience to the pontiff, the "representative of Jesus on earth, head of the Catholic Church."

For two weeks Mrs. Sung appeared in St. Peter's Square every morning to pray for a while. She also underwent a pregnancy test at a nearby institution, and afterward regretfully announced that she was not expecting a child by the archbishop. She was visibly losing weight and getting weak. The media were delighted.

Fearing a public relations debacle, the Vatican asked the South Korean ambassador to the Holy See to persuade Mrs. Sung to end the hunger strike and agree to some sort of accommodation. She refused to accept a handwritten letter from the archbishop and insisted on meeting with him.

Archbishop Milingo, supposedly still on a spiritual retreat, made an unannounced appearance on Italian state TV and said he had decided to stay in the Roman Catholic Church. When the television interviewer asked him whether he still loved Mrs. Sung, he said he loved her "like a sister." In a separate TV program a churchman who had once been Milingo's superior in the Curia and had remained a friend, Cardinal Giovanni Cheli, declared himself convinced that the whole affair was "the work of the Demon [Satan]."

After long, secret negotiations, a meeting between Archbishop Milingo and Mrs. Sung was at last arranged. Elaborate strategies kept the media at bay: the Korean woman was spirited out of her hotel, hidden in a sport utility vehicle, and taken to another hotel, the Arcangelo a few city blocks from the Vatican. Milingo arrived a little later in a Vatican limousine, escorted by papal and Italian security officers.

The archbishop and Mrs. Sung stayed together for three hours, always in the presence of other people. Milingo read her a letter to "my dear sister, Maria Sung," restating his commitment to the Catholic Church and its rule of celibacy. He promised to pray for Mrs. Sung every day of his life and assured her that God's benediction would stay with her. The farewell letter, whose text was later released by the Vatican, oddly ended with a businesslike "Sincerely, Archbishop E. Milingo." Breathless reporters caught up with the archbishop when he was leaving the Arcangelo Hotel; Mrs. Sung had already left.

Eyewitnesses to the encounter said that the archbishop and Mrs. Sung had been crying, and Mrs. Sung said she would never remarry. She ended her hunger strike and, together with Milingo, ate a supper of boiled rice and tofu. A few days later she and her entourage of the Unification Church left for New York.

Italian media commentators estimated that the Rome trip by Mrs. Sung and her escorts had cost Reverend Moon's organization at least $25,000—money well spent on a publicity coup.

While the pope and Vatican officials were pondering which role Archbishop Milingo should henceforth play in the church, conservative curialists were understood to be muttering that he had received particularly lenient treatment: other clerics who had similarly violated their vows had been dealt with much more sternly by church authorities. Was the rule of celibacy optional for certain prelates?

That high ecclesiastical rank doesn't prevent sentimental attachments and emotional conflicts is also shown by Esther's story. She came to Rome from a Western country to study social communications on a scholarship. She was aiming for a media career—possibly as a television reporter, editor, or producer—and was happy to obtain a part-time job at Vatican Radio, thanks to a recommendation by a Jesuit priest back home.

Since she is something of a linguist, Vatican Radio used her from time to time as an announcer or translator, and every now and then as an interviewer. One day her department chief asked her to interview a bishop from her own country who was attending the synod in the Vatican, and gave her an outline of the kind of questions she should ask him—mostly on how to handle pastoral work among new immigrants.

Esther prepared herself carefully for the interview, writing out the questions she would ask, learning them by heart, and saying them aloud a few times until she thought she sounded spontaneous and natural. As it happened, the bishop proved to be articulate, and Esther departed from her script a few times to follow up what he had been saying. The bishop was in his mid-fifties (she had checked him out in the Vatican yearbook), with a full head of graying hair and metal-rimmed spectacles, slightly pudgy.

The interview was recorded in one of the studios of Vatican Radio headquarters and was broadcast one evening a few days later. Esther's department chief told her that she had done a good job and that the bishop was very happy with it.

. . .

The synod of bishops is a consultative assembly that was made into a periodic event after the Second Vatican Council, to give the hierarchy at large, and through it the rank and file of the church, a chance of being heard by the pope and the Roman Curia. It was meant as a step toward what in Roman Catholicism is called collegiality, the theory that the church is governed by the pope together with the bishops (although in practice the pontiff remains the supreme legislator, ruler, and judge).

It is the pope alone who sets the date for a synod—usually every few years—and draws up its agenda. National and regional bishops' conferences elect representatives to the assembly in the Vatican; they spend about a month (possibly October) in Rome. The synod is attended by about a hundred delegates from local churches as well as by scores of cardinals and other officials of the Roman Curia.

For Vatican Radio a synod presents a welcome opportunity to enliven its programs by letting participating bishops discuss religious, social, and cultural problems in their own dioceses and countries. A few days after the interview that Esther had conducted, she found a note at Vatican Radio headquarters asking her to call the bishop between seven and eight P.M. at the national college where he was staying during his sojourn in Rome.

Esther called, and the bishop asked her a favor: could she get him a tape of the interview? He knew, he said, he could obtain it through channels, but he was busy with synod affairs all day, and maybe she could help. Esther promised to try, spoke to her department chief, and eventually had the tape and a transcript of the interview.

She called the college again, got the bishop on the phone,

and offered to drop off the tape and transcript at the institution. "Why don't we meet in St. Peter's Square instead, and let's have dinner together," the bishop suggested. Esther said yes.

The following evening she didn't immediately recognize her interviewee because he had come in a simple dark suit with a dark blue necktie. It was he who first spotted her in the piazza, which was slowly emptying of people. There was no sign that he was an ecclesiastic; maybe he had worn a cross on his lapel when he had left the college after changing into street clothes, and had removed it later.

Esther thought the bishop would take her to some refectory in the Vatican; she had never been inside and didn't know what it offered. Instead, the bishop asked her, "Do you know Trastevere?" Living in Rome, she had of course been to a couple of trattorias in the folksy-fashionable neighborhood on the right bank of the Tiber, downstream of the Vatican. The bishop said he had had a good dinner with Curia officials at a nice place there and had liked it very much; would she mind?

There were still cabs in the taxi stand just outside St. Peter's Square, and the two drove to the Trastevere trattoria. By Roman standards, they were very early and easily found an outside table in the narrow lane where only pedestrians and, alas, plenty of noisy motor scooters could pass. The bishop asked Esther to advise him on food and wine, and she suggested the pasta house specialty and Frascati. "Blond Frascati, the Romans say," Esther informed the bishop. He drank a lot of it.

When the inevitable flower vendor, a dark-skinned man who looked like a Gypsy, accosted their table, the bishop bought a small bunch of roses, paying a price that Esther found horrendous without haggling, as a Roman would. *My God, he's flirting with me!* Esther thought as the bishop smilingly presented the flowers to her, bowing slightly.

During their meal the bishop questioned her closely about her background, her studies, her Vatican Radio job, and her plans for the future. An elderly violinist and a young crooner turned up, serenading the alfresco diners with Roman and Neapolitan songs. "Ah, la dolce vita!" the bishop sighed, and gave the musicians a big tip.

Over the fancy cup of ice cream that was their dessert after the pasta and seafood, the bishop asked Esther: "Wouldn't you like to join my diocesan staff? We need an expert public relations person, and I plan to develop our own radio and maybe television service. You would be just the right choice for such a job. We can pay a good salary and have a benefits and pension plan for our lay employees. And the diocese could get you living quarters; we own some real estate."

Esther said sagaciously that she was more than honored by such a tempting offer but would first like to earn a Roman degree. "You can easily get your degree from one of our institutions of higher education," the bishop said. "Don't say yes or no now; think it over carefully and let's meet again before I leave for home."

At the bishop's request, Esther gave him the telephone number of the modest pensione where she was living. During the cab ride he took her hand—nothing more. He returned to his college in the same taxi after dropping her off at her pensione.

During the next few days the bishop called a few times, "just to say hello," and left friendly messages whenever she was out. They did meet again two days before the bishop was scheduled to fly home, and went again to the trattoria in the Trastevere district. That time the bishop didn't drink so much of the Frascati, and looked sad. "My life has changed since I met you, Esther," he said. "You can't imagine how lonely a bishop is. If I were free, I'd ask you to marry me. I don't suggest we have an affair, but I really would enjoy seeing you often and working with you and starting you on an interesting career course."

Esther said she hadn't yet spoken to her parents but would do so and surely think about his offer very carefully. "I'll call you from time to time," the bishop said. When he dropped her off at her pensione, he gave her a shy peck on the cheek.

During the following weeks the bishop called several times to ask whether she had made up her mind. "We'd have a nice, small apartment for you," he told her. Esther didn't really consult with her parents but just announced to them that she'd soon come home to take a good job with the diocese. At the end of the winter semester she left Rome. Months later she wrote to a friend that she enjoyed her new work and that her experience at Vatican Radio had been very useful.

Esther's Roman friend who is the main source of the foregoing account is convinced that she has "started an intimate relationship of some kind with her bishop."

VII

HOLY SEE HOME LIFE

The roughly eight hundred people living permanently or semipermanently in the State of Vatican City include the pope, his secretaries, and housekeepers; dozens of active or retired cardinals; many other ecclesiastics and nuns; and more than a hundred members of the Pontifical Swiss Guard as well as other security personnel. Furthermore, a number of lay employees and their families dwell in some building inside or right outside the walls surrounding the midget state. Another few hundred people—clerical and lay—have living quarters in various extraterritorial Vatican dependencies in various parts of Rome and its surroundings.

Vatican wives, in addition to doing domestic chores and helping bring up their children, may themselves commute to some job in Rome that has nothing to do with the church. Vatican youngsters go to school outside the papal enclave. The

Vatican has its own modernly equipped health service on three floors of a building facing the pharmacy and the Annona. Nearly twenty physicians, all men, take turns between their service in Italian hospitals or their private practices to be available in the Vatican. Papal employees must undergo medical tests once a year to make sure they are in reasonably good health. Lay dependents who miss more than two days of work must be examined in their own homes by a Vatican doctor unless they are in a hospital.

Residents of Vatican City who need clinical treatment are taken to some institution on Italian territory, as was Pope John Paul II after the attempt on his life in 1981, and again later for various ills. He was the first pontiff in history to be admitted to a public hospital—the Agostino Gemelli clinic, which is the teaching hospital of the well-regarded medical school of the Catholic University of the Sacred Heart on Monte Mario, one and a half miles northwest of the Vatican.

When Pope Paul VI required prostate surgery in 1967, clinical equipment was moved into the Apostolic Palace and a team of doctors and nurses were brought in to operate on him. Today there is a medical-emergency unit above the papal suite.

Holy See dependents receive their mail through the Vatican post office. Many other Romans also use the papal postal service, deemed more reliable than Italy's, but can do so only for outgoing mail, which must carry Vatican stamps. (Issuing ever newer series of well-designed stamps, which are at once snapped up by collectors around the world, is a minor Vatican moneymaker.)

The Vatican state shares its telephone area code with Rome and its country code with Italy: 39-06. Punch 39-06-6982 and the voice of a nun staffing the pontifical switchboard answers, "*Vaticano.*"

Residents of Vatican City will slip out in the evening to

go to one of the movie theaters or trattorias in the neighbor-hood or to visit friends. They must be back by midnight. The curfew is compulsory for ecclesiastics, Swiss Guards, and lay-people alike. The Gate of St. Anne on the Viale Angelico on the east side of Vatican City, through which most of everyday traffic moves, remains open until that hour; the other major entrances—the Bronze Door and the Archway of the Bells—close earlier. For emergencies there is a rarely used all-night passage, secured by Swiss Guards, on the left side of St. Peter's Square, near the Archway of the Bells.

Denizens of Vatican City generally are not allowed to keep pets, although there seems to be no objection to small, caged birds. (Pope Pius XII was fond of his canaries and other war-blers.) Permission for a cat may be obtained. I have seen felines prowling the Vatican Gardens; they probably had penetrated from outside the walls, criminally attracted by the many birds that regard the papal park, and especially its small forested patch, as their own sanctuary.

For years I had a friend living in the Vatican, Professor Cesidio Lolli, deputy editor in chief of *L'Osservatore Romano*. Whenever I visited him at his apartment next to his office in the north of the enclave, his wife seemed to be in bed suffering from one of her frequent painful attacks of arthritis.

One day Lolli told me, still gripped by emotion, that in the preceding afternoon he had answered the doorbell and to his utter surprise and confusion found Pope John XXIII standing outside, all alone. "How's Signora Lolli?" the pontiff asked. Lolli sank to his knees and kissed the pontifical ring. John XXIII stepped into Mrs. Lolli's sickroom, sat at her bedside awhile, and prayed with her. "We both were so overcome that we could hardly speak," Lolli recalled. The papal surprise visit was not mentioned in *L'Osservatore Romano* nor in any other newspaper.

Perpetuity

The pope and his closest entourage live in a twenty-room apartment—including a private chapel with pews for forty-six worshipers—on the fourth floor of the Apostolic Palace. To Italians this is the third story because they don't count the ground floor; when you hear in the Vatican that some request or order comes "direct from the third floor," it means from the pope himself or from his live-in aides.

Ever since Pope John Paul II's election in 1978, five sisters of the Congregation of the Servants of the Sacred Heart of Jesus of Kraków have lived with him on a rotating basis. Few people have ever seen them; their existence in Rome resembles that of cloistered nuns. They cook the Polish and Italian dishes that the pope likes—he is particularly fond of desserts—and serve at his table when he has guests. John Paul II loves company at his meals and regularly invites visiting bishops from all over the world, theologians, curial officials, friends from Poland, and the occasional layman or -woman to have breakfast after mass in his private chapel, or lunch or dinner with him. Whenever there are no outsiders, the sisters sit down at the pontiff's table. They substitute for the family that John Paul II never had; one of them, Sister Eufrosyna, also acts as a confidential secretary, answering his personal mail.

Italians call the female housekeeper of a cleric *la perpetua*. You will also hear more than one non-Italian prelate familiarly and jocularly speak of "my *perpetua*," a woman taking care of his domestic establishment. The term seems to suggest an everlasting relationship that is impossible in a world of mortals but at any rate conveys the notion of long service.

Actually, Perpetua is the given name of a minor personage in the novel *The Betrothed* by Alessandro Manzoni (1785–1873), an Italian classic with which the nation's students are relentlessly tortured during their high school years. Quotes from *The Betrothed* dot Italian newspaper prose and parliamentary rhetoric all the time. The work, in the manner of Sir Walter Scott, is set in the turbulent period of the seventeenth century when petty lords oppressed Lombardy between raids by pillaging soldiery on the fringes of the Thirty Years' War in the north and when a catastrophic plague devastated Spanish-ruled Milan.

Perpetua doesn't have much space in the rich tapestry of Manzoni's romantic novel, but readers remember her as the voice of populist common sense. She is the housekeeper of a pusillanimous parson, Don Abbondio—a domineering servant who talks back to her master, arms on her hips, with little respect but not without affection. Made of much more robust stuff than the weak priest, she knows everything about his problems and fears. When marauders invade their village and parsonage, the two flee to Milan, where Perpetua dies of the plague but the fainthearted cleric survives.

Manzoni describes Perpetua as having "passed the synodal age of forty years, remaining unmarried." Synods at various times decreed that women employed in the households of priests must have passed the child-bearing age (also called the canonical age), assumed to be about forty years.

Quite a few women of course give birth in their early or mid-forties, and menopause in most women sets in well after the age of forty. The 1983 version of the Code of Canon Law in its Canon 277 merely says that "clerics are obliged to observe perfect and perpetual continence for the sake of the Kingdom of Heaven and therefore are bound to celibacy, which is a special gift of God. . . . Clerics are to behave with due prudence towards persons whose company can endanger their obligation to observe continence or give rise to scandal among the faithful." This may apply to male servants and friends, too.

Rephrasing much older norms, the 1917 Code of Canon Law, superseded by the 1983 revision, had been much more specific: it enjoined priests to avoid "cohabitation" with women who might cause suspicion of "something evil." Canon 133 of the church's 1917 lawbook had advised clerics that their mothers, a sister, an aunt, or some virtuous elderly woman might conveniently do domestic chores for them.

Today visitors may see female servants who are in their thirties or even younger in the households of Vatican prelates. Some of the Polish nuns in John Paul II's household don't seem to be advanced in years, either. The canonical-age rule appears to have been quietly dropped.

A few earlier popes also had female housekeepers, but Pius XI, the former Achille Ratti, upon his election to the pontifical throne deemed it unseemly to bring his *perpetua* of many years from Milan, where he had been archbishop. As Siora Teodolinda (*Siora* being Milanese dialect for *Signora*, "Mrs."), she had won notoriety because of her outspokenness. She had also been with the future pontiff when he was apostolic nuncio to Poland after World War I. Pius XI called Franciscan friars to replace Teodolinda, although their cooking skills were presumably no match for hers. Desolate, she obtained refuge in a convent near St. Peter's in Rome, to be at least near her former master and see him during public ceremonies from time to time.

Pius XI's successor, Pius XII, on the other hand, wouldn't do without *his* housekeeper, the formidable Sister Pascalina, even during the conclave that resulted in his election. Pascalina became one of the most powerful Vatican personages during his nineteen-year pontificate (see chapter 2).

Pope John XXIII, who was fond of good, wholesome cuisine, used to discuss the day's lunch and dinner menus with a group of Poor Sisters of Bergamo who kept house for him, enjoying the few moments of chatting with them in their own

Venetian dialect. The person who was closest to him was his earnest secretary, Monsignor Loris Capovilla, who hailed from a small town near Bergamo and after his pontifical master's death was to be put in charge of the shrine of Loreto and later the diocese of Chieti. Eventually, as a titular archbishop, he would retire to John XXIII's birthplace, the village of Sotto il Monte, near Bergamo.

Pope Paul VI brought with him from Milan a coterie of intellectuals with artistic tastes—priests and a few laymen—who were soon labeled the "Milan Mafia" by Vatican gossip. He had no woman housekeeper. His private secretary, Monsignor Pasquale Macchi, hovered around the pontiff and, because of his influence and protective attitude, was compared with the unforgotten Pascalina. At Paul VI's side, as always, during a papal trip to East Asia, Australia, and Samoa in 1970, he threw himself between his master and a knife-wielding Bolivian assailant at Manila Airport, probably saving Paul VI's life. After Paul VI's death Macchi, too, was put in charge of the shrine of Loreto for some time and was promoted to archbishop.

When Pope John Paul I unexpectedly died only thirty-three days after his election in 1978, the Vatican said at first that he had been found lifeless in his bed by the Reverend John Magee, an Irishman who served as his translator and secretary (and later was to become bishop of Cloyne, Ireland). Only later did the Vatican reluctantly change its story: Sister Vincenza Taffarel, who had been with the pontiff ever since he was bishop of Vittorio Veneto, had penetrated the papal bedroom when she noticed that a cup of coffee that, as usual, she had put outside the door had remained untouched. That a woman might enter the pontiff's bedroom clearly had made the Vatican spin doctors uncomfortable.

Princely Households

Once known as "princes of the church," cardinals in past centuries truly lived in aristocratic splendor. Some were members of noble families, such as the Colonna and Orsini of Rome, the Medici of Florence, the Borgia of Spain, and the Rohan of France. Each one a potential successor to the reigning pope, they resided in their own palaces and had their own courtlike establishments with secretaries, chaplains, stewards, men-at-arms, buffoons, maybe a personal astrologer, and hangers-on. Quite a few members of what until a short time ago was called the Sacred College kept mistresses or patronized artists, or both. In conclave, during the Renaissance era some twenty cardinals, the majority of them Italians and many of them residing in Rome, would elect a new pope.

In the early twentieth century, when the number of cardinals had gradually risen to seventy, all were still expected to live in some distinguished, detached building with a porte cochere and to travel in a separate first-class railroad compartment. Nowadays cardinals fly business class, possibly with traveling corporate executives or fashion models as seat neighbors.

Quite a few of the current cardinals are older than eighty years of age and therefore, under a reform enacted by Pope Paul VI in 1970, no longer qualified to take part in a conclave for the election of a new head of the church. Of the fifty or so cardinals residing in Rome at any given time, several serve as heads of curial departments or hold other high positions; the remainder are semiretired or fully retired. Each is entitled to his own apartment in the Vatican or in a Vatican-owned building outside the pontifical state and is free to make his own household arrangements. Transportation is provided daily or on request by the Vatican car pool.

Calling at the residence of a member of the Cardinalitial

College—this clumsy expression has officially replaced the old term, Sacred College—is usually still a formal affair. If the cardinal lives in one of the stately buildings on Italian soil just outside St. Peter's Square, as some do, you have to know the number of his apartment: the list of tenants at the street entrance near the intercom carries no names, just figures. Press the appropriate button and state your name; if you have an appointment, the entrance door will spring open and you may take the elevator to His Eminence's floor.

You will usually be received by a butler or a nun. In the hall you will see a scarlet biretta on a shelf or a little table; it is one of the cardinal's badges, first put on his head ceremonially in public consistory by the pope who elevated him. There will be a private chapel where His Eminence says mass every morning; his study and library; a parlor; his private bedroom and bath; and the quarters of his housekeepers, usually at least a couple of nuns; and probably a wardrobe room to hold his manifold liturgical vestments and everyday clothes.

A cardinal who entertains a lot (many do) will keep his household staff quite busy. A nun who took care of the late American cardinal John J. Wright, who was head of the Vatican's congregation for Bishops, was renowned for the elaborate cakes she baked. Other members of the College of Cardinals would angle for lunch or dinner invitations, or even borrow their colleague's confectioner-nun for their own parties. Cardinals invite one another all the time.

Archbishops and bishops in Vatican service do not live quite as sumptuously as cardinals, but comfortably enough, often in Vatican buildings and usually with female housekeepers.

A mere monsignor who works for the Vatican may find a nun with some cooking skills sufficient for his needs, or he may take his meals at some convent or other church institution near his living quarters and have a Filipina maid, shared with a colleague, come in for housework a few hours every other day.

Gossip reaching prelates by way of the Vatican supermarket and their housekeepers is often useful. An archbishop who had just proudly shown off his new upper-floor digs with a large terrace in a Vatican-owned apartment near St. Peter's Square confided: "Sister Emilia, who just let you in, is responsible for our now living here. She had long set her eyes on this place, and so had I. When she learned at the Annona that the previous tenant—poor man, he was sick—was taking a turn for the worse, I hurried to APSA and put in for his apartment, just in case. He died late last year. APSA paid for the most urgent repairs, and I pitched in with my own money and a loan from my brother for a dishwasher and other improvements."

Vatican personnel, both clerical and lay, usually get preference as tenants, often at favorable terms, in APSA-controlled buildings. An unmarried woman employee of the Vatican who several years ago started as a secretary and more recently was given a mid-level job said: "I still live in a small place a half-hour ride in two buses from the Vatican, with the rent taking up almost half of my salary. For more than a year I have been going to the APSA office in the Apostolic Palace every week, pressing them to assign me one of their apartments. They let me see four or five different places, mostly of the studio type, and told me I'd have to pay for making them livable myself. I told the archbishop in charge that I knew APSA also had better apartments, although I didn't presume to have a suite like a cardinal; I had heard that one nice place had recently been rented by a bank official who doesn't belong to Vatican personnel. The archbishop denied this but seemed embarrassed." The frustrated house hunter had got the information from a nun who did domestic chores for a monsignor.

To the member of a religious order for women, looking after the well-being and the living quarters of a cardinal or other high ecclesiastic is generally more exciting than staying in a convent under the direct control of the mother superior and in constant company of sisters whom she may dislike.

A prelate's household help attend the mass he says in his chapel every morning, see other churchmen and laypeople who are their boss's visitors or guests at meals, and pick up interesting snatches of conversation. They may eat at their master's table whenever he doesn't entertain. They hear about the prelate's family affairs if a relative comes to bring news from back home or to ask a favor. They know about their master's mannerisms, guess his moods, and remind him of the medications he has to take. For quite a few ecclesiastics, a *perpetua* becomes a wife substitute.

Religious orders, on the other hand, usually like to place one or more of their members in the household of a Vatican personage. Such a connection fosters prestige and may prove useful whenever the order needs guidance and help in the meanders of the Curia. There are some two thousand orders of nuns and sisters (the distinction is vague) among the big families of religious women—Franciscans, Benedictines, Dominicans, and others—and smaller congregations and communities. New groups spring up all the time, seeking recognition by the Curia's Congregation for Institutes of Consecrated Life and Societies of Apostolic Life. Such newcomers to female monasticism often try to place one or more of their members in the household of a Vatican prelate as a shortcut to the Curia.

A Latin American monsignor who had been ordained in Rome and had been called back to the Vatican after several years' service in his home diocese said: "Without Sister Antonia, I couldn't function here. I call her 'Sister,' but she isn't really a nun. She belongs to an Association of Familiars of the Clergy." This is neither a religious organization nor a labor union; it's a network of unmarried or widowed women who take care of priestly households.

"Sister" Antonia was recommended to the monsignor by a colleague in the Curia. A bishop for whom she had worked for more than ten years had died, and as she didn't want to rejoin her family in a small southern Italian town, she was looking for a new position. "She is a real professional," her new master said. "The first thing she did was to go through my wardrobe and fasten loose buttons and launder and press surplices. She keeps the small apartment tidy and puts the food that I like on the table—rice, pasta, and lots of vegetables. She dusts my books, although she tends to misplace them. On weekends I work in a parish on the outskirts to help the pastor, and when I come home, Sister Antonia regularly is watching soccer on TV. She is an avid fan of Lazio [a soccer team], as her bishop was, and I'm afraid I am beginning to root for Lazio myself."

It sounded like a middle-class, middle-aged marital idyll. The clerical friend of the monsignor who had introduced him to his housekeeper commented later: "That Antonia really bosses the good monsignor. She wants him to become a bishop."

Murky Matters

The families living in the State of Vatican City included for years that of Ercole Orlandi, a messenger of the Prefecture of the Apostolic Household. Today the main task of that old and influential office is to regulate and schedule papal audiences.

Applications to meet the head of the church pour into the Vatican by the hundreds every week from bishops, priests, laypersons, politicians, diplomats, members of other faiths, and even nonbelievers. The Prefecture of the Apostolic Household sifts through them, consulting with the Secretariat of State, other Curia departments, and the pontiff's private secretaries; if the application is granted, the prefecture assigns a time slot for the audience. Mr. Orlandi used to deliver formal admission cards to applicants who might reside in a hotel or at a private address, or had to be contacted through an embassy. The papal messenger's job requires a dignified bearing, discretion, and reliability. He has to be available on short notice, and for that reason Mr. Orlandi lived with his wife and their five children in a Vatican service apartment.

On June 22, 1983, their daughter Emanuela, fifteen years old, disappeared mysteriously. She has never been found. Search posters disseminated around Rome during the following days and weeks gave her height as 1.60 meters (five foot three) and said she had long, straight black hair and on the day she vanished was wearing blue jeans, a white shirt, and gym shoes. A portrait on the poster shows a smiling adolescent with a headband, her dark hair falling to her shoulders, looking a little older than her stated age, pleasant but not beautiful.

Emanuela—who was a Vatican citizen, as were the other members of her family—had left her home in the papal state one afternoon to attend a flute lesson at a private music school near the building of the Italian Senate, in the historic center of Rome. Two policemen on guard duty outside the upper house of the Italian parliament stated later that they had noticed a girl who fit Emanuela's description at approximately five P.M. with a well-dressed, baldish man, about thirty-five years old. At 7:20 P.M. Emanuela called home, telling her older sister, Federica, that she had meant to ask their mother's permission to distribute publicity handbills for a cosmetics firm; a man had approached her, promising she would be paid for the little job. Emanuela remarked to her sister that she would like to pick up a little pocket money. The girls' mother wasn't home, having accompanied her youngest daughter, Cristina, to a dance rehearsal in another central neighborhood.

That phone call apparently was the last sign of life from the missing girl. Her parents turned to the Italian police, who at first assumed that Emanuela had run off the way quite a few teenagers do all the time. Her relatives declared that they never believed this—Emanuela wouldn't do such a thing. Eventually the police opened a formal missing-person investigation, and the family had the search posters put up and started inquiries of their own, keeping in touch with the police.

During the following weeks and months, the Orlandis got several phone calls from people introducing themselves by various names, claiming to know Emanuela's whereabouts; some seemed to know details of the girl's person and life. No further contacts could, however, be established.

Eventually a caller who said he was an American asserted that Emanuela had been kidnapped and that he was her guard. The "American" offered to free her in exchange for the release from jail of Mehmet Ali Agca, the Turkish gunman who in May 1981 had fired on Pope John Paul II in St. Peter's Square, gravely wounding him. Other messages from different sources later also linked Emanuela's disappearance with the 1981 attempt on the pontiff's life.

Finally Ali Agca himself got into the act from the high-security prison where he was serving a life sentence. He declared that Emanuela was alive and that secret operatives had organized her kidnapping to get him freed. The prisoner, however, had lied so often in the past that his statement was met with disbelief; attempts to verify it led nowhere.

Later an Italian, Francesco Pio Sbrocchi, was detained on a charge of attempted fraud by trying to get money out of the Vatican, claiming he was able to solve the Emanuela Orlandi mystery: she was living with a boss of the Neapolitan *camorra* (a bunch of local criminal gangs) and had a five-year-old child. Then there were rumors that she was in a convent in Brazil. The subtext: she had had an affair with an influential cleric and had been spirited away.

All supposed leads proved futile. Various Italian officials complained that they had received scant cooperation from the Vatican in their missing-person investigation. The Rome judiciary closed the unsolved case fourteen years after Emanuela had vanished.

It is doubtful that Pope John Paul II mentioned the Emanuela Orlandi affair when he visited his assailant in a Rome prison in 1984 to signify that he had forgiven the Turk. The two spoke alone in Agca's cell—probably bugged—for some time.

In 2000 the president of Italy, yielding to strong pressure by the pontiff, issued a pardon for Agca as a gesture of heeding the Vatican's appeal for a general amnesty program during the church's Millennium Jubilee. In June of that year the Turk was extradited to his homeland, where another isolation cell in a high-security prison near Istanbul and another string of penal proceedings were awaiting him.

In all the years since the assault in St. Peter's Square, the Italian police and judiciary have never been able to determine Agca's motives and who, if anybody, had assisted him. Many conspiracy theories have been bandied about, with the case of Emanuela Orlandi again and again tied in, although in 1997 a Roman prosecutor had ruled out any connection.

After Ali Agca left Italy, a former magistrate who likes media exposure, Ferdinando Imposimato, declared himself convinced that Emanuela Orlandi had been abducted by the Grey Wolves—a Turkish right-wing terrorist organization to which Agca is believed to have belonged—to bring about his liberation. Mr. Imposimato asserted that Emanuela was alive and might soon return home. She didn't.

If Emanuela were alive, she would have been thirty-four years old at the time. On various occasions her relatives have expressed their hope, even their near certainty, that Emanuela was living somewhere and that they would hear from her at some future date.

The family had moved out of the Vatican after Mr. Orlandi's retirement. One of Emanuela's brothers, Pietro, obtained a good job at the Vatican bank, which is known as the Institute for the Works of Religion (IOR). This wasn't a special favor to the family; the descendants of many Vatican employees enter papal service. When the younger Mr. Orlandi was asked about his family's relations with the Holy See after his sister's disappearance, he said: "They were always close to us in prayer."

Another female resident of the Vatican became one of three victims in a grisly episode of bloodshed in 1998, the worst instance of violence in the pontifical state since the 1981 assassination attempt on Pope John Paul II. What actually happened has never been satisfactorily established.

At about nine P.M. on May 4, 1998, shots were heard in the building parallel to the barracks of the Pontifical Swiss Guards, north of the Apostolic Palace and St. Peter's Square. Vatican City at night is one of the quietest areas in Rome, although in the warm months when windows are open the sounds of television—not too loud!—may be heard from the living quarters of prelates and employees, and maybe a song or two from the Swiss Guard barracks.

The startling bangs that sounded like firecrackers appeared to have come from the service apartment of the Swiss Guards' commander. Vatican security men and neighbors entered the premises and found three dead bodies. They were Colonel

Alois Estermann, the commander; his wife, Gladys Meza Romero Estermann; and Vice Corporal Cédric Tornay.

The cardinal secretary of state, his closest aides, and eventually the pope himself were informed, and after ten P.M. the papal spokesman, Joaquin Navarro-Valls, was summoned to the Vatican from his apartment in a northeastern neighborhood across the Tiber. Dr. Navarro, who had specialized in psychiatry before becoming a journalist, was to play a leading role in the investigation of the events in the Swiss Guard commander's apartment in addition to managing the media.

A formal inquiry was the responsibility of an official with the title Sole Judge of the State of Vatican City, Gianluigi Marrone. Mr. Marrone—who as chief of personnel of the Italian Chamber of Deputies had dual Italian and Vatican citizenship—also served at the pontifical state's lower court for civil and penal cases not directly connected with ecclesiastical matters (which are the exclusive province or church jurisdiction). During the night of the Vatican drama, Mr. Marrone could not immediately be reached at his home outside the papal state. Italian newspapers would later quote him as admitting that he had no experience whatsoever with criminal cases. Italian authorities did not officially participate in any phase of the Vatican proceedings.

Dr. Navarro spent a good deal of the night of May 4 in the Vatican, and in the early morning briefed the media and Italian officials. Later in the day he held a press conference, repeating his first version of what had happened: Colonel Estermann and his wife were alone in their Vatican home shortly before nine P.M. on May 4 when the twenty-three-year-old vice corporal called at the door. Admitted to the apartment, Tornay fired five shots from a Swiss Army revolver, killing his commander and Mrs. Estermann and then turning the weapon on himself.

The papal spokesman asserted that the vice corporal had

acted in a "mad frenzy." The motives for the murder-suicide were "clear": Tornay had been repeatedly reprimanded by his commander and had been skipped over in the awards of papal decorations that were to be presented to other members of the Swiss Guards during the swearing-in of recruits in a ceremony to take place later that week.

The shooting in the Vatican caused a sensation and inevitably gave rise to a flood of rumors. It wouldn't be Rome if there hadn't been lurid speculation about what might have *really* caused the bloodbath—a love triangle? Insane jealousy? A homosexual liaison between the commander and the subaltern? A romantic affair suddenly broken off? A conspiracy?

Colonel Estermann, forty-four years old, had been appointed commander of the Swiss Guards shortly before his death. He had been a major in the army of Switzerland before enrolling in papal service as a simple halberdier (private) in 1980. The lanky Swiss had been at John Paul II's side as a security guard in plain clothes on May 13, 1981, when Mehmet Ali Agca fired at the pope, who was riding in an open car in St. Peter's Square. Estermann caught the pontiff, who was bleeding profusely, in his arms and, together with other aides, carried him into the ambulance that had quickly been called.

Estermann later rose through the ranks and accompanied John Paul II as a bodyguard on many of his far-flung pastoral journeys. He became deputy commander of the Swiss Guards, with the rank of a major, and on the retirement of his superior, Colonel Roland Buchs, succeeded him as a colonel and new commander.

He had met his wife in Rome, where they were married in 1983. Mrs. Estermann, born in Venezuela, was forty-eight years old at the time of her death. She was tall, dark-haired, and attractive, a university graduate who had been a fashion model and then a policewoman in her native country. She had a job at the Venezuelan embassy to the Holy See and was commuting to its offices beyond the Tiber every working day. The Estermanns were childless.

Vice Corporal Tornay, the presumed murderer, came from a French-speaking village in the canton Valais. Colonel Estermann was reported to have rebuked him in writing for violating the service regulations by staying out of the barracks one night and to have told him that he should look for another job because he would probably be dismissed.

Colonel Estermann was to pin the medals to the elaborate Renaissance uniforms of the honorees—skipping Tornay—during the traditional ceremony held in the Vatican every May 6. New guardsmen were to be sworn in on that occasion, too.

The annual rite commemorates the Swiss mercenaries who died defending Pope Clement VII on May 6, 1527. On that day the troops of Emperor Charles V, who had conquered Rome, ran wild, looting, raping, and killing—even threatening the life of the pontiff. The commander of the Switzers, Kaspar Roist, was one of the 147 who gave their lives to cover Clement VII's escape from the Vatican to safety in the Castel Sant'Angelo, the papal fortress on the Tiber.

After the shooting of May 4, 1998, the Swiss Guard rite was canceled in a gesture of mourning; it was held in a subdued mood a few weeks later. Masses were said in the Vatican for the Estermanns and for their alleged murderer.

Vice Corporal Tornay, it was unofficially learned, had given one of his comrades a letter for his mother in Switzerland an hour before he called on his commander on May 4. Its exact wording has never been made public; it was said to uphold the version that the Vatican spokesman had provided a few hours after the shooting and well before the outcome of the postmortems (if they were performed at all) were known and the Vatican inquiry was concluded.

Eventually the Vatican announced that the Sole Judge had confirmed the spokesman's statements: The vice corporal had acted in a state of mental derangement. His findings were later upheld by the Court of Appeals of the State of Vatican City, whose justices are all clerics.

Italian media voiced astonishment at the Vatican's brisk procedures in the wake of a tragedy that resulted in three people killed. Since it had occurred on the territory of the sovereign pontifical state, no interference by outsiders was possible. Many Romans say to this day that the Vatican acted with undue haste to close the case without an exhaustive investigation and failed to inform the public of all the facts that must have emerged.

Even if the official Vatican explanation of what happened is accepted, one question remains unanswered: Why did the vice corporal, if he was frenzied by hatred of his commander, also murder Mrs. Estermann, whom he could hardly have known?

If Tornay had survived, the Vatican might not have known what to do with him, although it claims to exercise full judicial powers regarding crimes occurring on its territory. When the Turk, Ali Agca, made the attempt on the life of Pope John Paul II in 1981, he was arrested by Italian police in St. Peter's Square and taken to an Italian prison. The square is part of the State of Vatican City, but Italian police are allowed to patrol it because it is wide open to the adjoining Roman neighborhood. The papal state made no request for extradition of the would-be assassin and clearly didn't want to try him.

The Vatican's record in dealing with criminal cases is spotty; it does have a minuscule prison, but most of the time its single cell is used as a storeroom. In a farcical episode in the 1950s, a young monsignor who was held in the Vatican's Tower of Winds for alleged fraud locked his warden in his own prison and nonchalantly walked out of the papal territory. Some time later the Italian police discovered and detained him in the apartment of a woman friend of his. The cleric, an official of the Vatican Secretariat of State who was alleged to have been mixed up with illegal foreign-currency transactions and ruinous movie-picture deals, was sentenced to nine years' imprisonment by an Italian court. He was cleared on appeal. The Vatican had unfrocked him but after a number of years readmitted him to the priesthood but didn't restore his rank as a monsignor.

VIII

VOICES FROM THE VATICAN

Sister Johanna is the housekeeper of an Italian cardinal in his early eighties who has retired from a high position in the Curia but continues to live in his six-room apartment in a Vatican-owned building a stone's throw from St. Peter's Square. She is really a trained nurse from the Trentino region who years ago helped look after the cardinal in a church-affiliated hospital in Rome when he was recovering from stomach surgery.

The cardinal's former housekeeper, a German woman, had decided she wanted to go home, so he implored Sister Johanna to fill the void in his household. Experienced nurses are in much demand, yet the cardinal got Sister Johanna a leave of absence from the hospital and, with a couple of phone calls to her mother superior, obtained permission for the nursing sister to become his *perpetua* for six months—shorter if he were to find a replacement sooner. Sister Johanna can't remember ever having been asked whether she wanted the job.

The six months have meanwhile become more than four years. The cardinal is on a rigid diet since his operation, and Sister Johanna, who is forty-two, has no trouble fixing breakfast and two bland meals for him every day and keeping his clothes and apartment in reasonable order. She vacuums the place daily ("there is an incredible amount of dust in the Roman air"), and whenever she needs help for moving the refrigerator or heavy furniture, she by now knows how to get someone from the Vatican's labor force for a few hours. Although she would like to return to nursing at the hospital, the cardinal won't let her go.

Since his retirement the cardinal has little to do. He accepts almost every invitation to some diplomatic reception or ceremony but has dropped out of the clerical lunch-and-dinner circuit because of his diet. He trusts only Sister Johanna's cooking, which is simple enough—"boring food," she says. Nor does the cardinal ever entertain any guests, except maybe someone from his old office—now headed by a younger cardinal—for a cup of tea. The cardinal suspects the number two man in that department, an archbishop, of scheming to get the top job and his apartment one day. After he had the archbishop for tea last time, the cardinal muttered to Sister Johanna: "He was looking around all over the place, and I had the feeling that while we talked he was figuring where he would put his furniture and stuff and what changes he would make. I half expected him to whip out a tape measure."

Sister Johanna serves at mass, which the cardinal says at seven A.M. every day, and then gives him breakfast. Almost every morning he sighs that not being allowed to drink coffee is "one of the greatest sacrifices in my old age." Sister Johanna brews coffee for herself in the kitchen, and the cardinal sometimes walks in just to smell it. "A noseful only," he will say.

Whenever there is a ceremony in St. Peter's or elsewhere to which retired cardinals are welcome, Sister Johanna lays out the appropriate vestments. She has learned what a prince of the church is expected to wear on which occasions. Usually the Secretariat of the Cardinalitial College issues guidelines, and Sister Johanna has become friendly with the housekeepers of other cardinals whom she can ask for advice.

Sister Johanna's congregation has some use for the cardinal: he visits their general headquarters on the outskirts of Rome once a week to say mass for the sisters and hear their confessions. Every now and then the mother superior needs either a recommendation from him or his personal intervention to solve some problem with the Curia. Sister Johanna's boss has, in effect, become the "cardinal protector" of her order, although that title no longer exists (the rationale being that mothers superior don't need an intermediary in their dealings with the Vatican bureaucracy).

"His Eminence is a very lonely man," Sister Johanna observes repeatedly. At night, after an early dinner that he eats alone, he usually asks her to watch the TV evening news with him. Often he points at some personage on the screen, saying, "I've met her," or "He's a real bastard." He also likes to pepper the news with sarcastic comments like "Yeah, destroy what little has remained of the school system." He has a low opinion of Italian politicians of any stripe. He always refers to the pope as the Holy Father and never says anything about him that may sound like criticism. However, he snorts when the cardinal secretary of state appears on screen.

The cardinal's only close relative is a widowed sister who lives near Genoa. She is too frail to travel to Rome, but the two talk by phone every three or four days, usually the sister being the one to call. Her two children, a son and a daughter, turn up at the cardinal's apartment whenever they need something, which is fairly often: admission to the Catholic University's medical school for one of the cardinal's great-nephews, maybe, or half a kilogram of the best Colombian coffee from the Annona, which Sister Johanna has to go get. She is convinced that the cardinal makes monetary gifts to his young relatives, although she doesn't think he has much cash.

What about Sister Johanna herself, does she feel lonely? Oh no, she is quick to reply. She keeps in touch with her former colleagues at the hospital by phone and sometimes sees them. She often goes back to her old convent, has coffee with other sisters, chats, prays, and sings with them. "If you are a *religiosa* [religious woman], you are never alone." What about her Vatican life? "The sisters at the convent think it must be great to be so close to the Holy Father, but they see him on television as I do in His Eminence's apartment. It was much more thrilling at the clinic."

A young woman, Olivia, who has a law degree and passed the bar examination after a period of practice in the joint law firm of her father and uncle was hired by the Vicariat, the office of the pope's cardinal vicar general for Rome. She does legal work connected with church property and with matters involving parishes and other ecclesiastical entities in Rome and its province.

"It's awfully dull," she says, "but it's relatively well paying. The church in Italy now has a lot of money, thanks to the eight per mille." She is referring to the 0.8 percent of residents' income taxes that they can earmark for the Roman Catholic Church or other denominations without increasing their own fiscal burden. Many Italian taxpayers do so, trusting that at least part of the money will go to charities and social work.

Yet Olivia doesn't want to handle real estate affairs—the bulk of her professional activities right now—all her life. She is working for a degree in canon law. "I want to be involved in Rota cases," she says. "It's mostly petitions for marriage annulments from everywhere in the world. Much more fun, and also more money."

She will have to register with the Roman Rota, one of the Vatican's tribunals, and attend a three-year course to become what is known as a Rotal advocate. Annulment cases would then be her main concern. Although divorce is legal in Catholic countries such as Italy and Poland, many Roman Catholics prefer to go through the church annulment process if they want to end their marriages, either by mutual agreement or unilaterally.

The way to do so is to petition the ecclesiastical court in one's own diocese. Its decision can be appealed to the regional church tribunal. If both levels of the ecclesiastical judiciary agree, the case is usually closed and the annulment granted. If a further appeal is filed by one of the parties, the Roman Rota has to decide; some cases, because of procedural quirks, go straight to the Rota, which may act as its own court of appeal by assigning a case that a three-man panel has handled to another of its panels.

"I read all the Rota decisions," Olivia says. "The names are omitted but you learn a lot about human nature and lawyers' skills. The church rejects divorce, and canon law doesn't recognize many reasons for annulment—just coercion, fright, error in the person of one's marriage partner, impotence, that sort of thing. If a couple have lived together for years and have kids, it will be hard to get an annulment, but it can be done. Such situations challenge the ingenuity of the Rotal advocate."

Maybe money helps, too, it was suggested to Olivia. She let the suggestion pass without comment, and went on: "Every year when the pope receives the judges of the Rota—more than twenty of them, and all men—he admonishes them to be strict in their application of church law, but they keep granting annulments nevertheless, even in some tough cases."

Italian state courts, Olivia explained, usually recognize Rotal decisions; many foreign judiciaries don't. What did she mean by what she said about human nature? Olivia was asked. "Reading the testimony, you sense as a lawyer that the principals or the witnesses were lying. Much of what's in the files has to do with bedroom matters, and to a woman often sounds highly unlikely. But the judges of the Rota, elderly monsignors all of them, may believe such stuff or feign to believe it. More and more of the Rotal advocates now are women, and their record for winning cases is good. I hope I never need one of them myself. My boyfriend, who is an architect, wants us to get married. 'If you get me to the altar by force or intimidation, it's reason for annulment,' I tell him."

Annamaria graduated from high school as a *ragioniera* (accountant) and was working part-time in a real estate agency in Rome when her favorite uncle, a priest who had once held a job in the Vatican administration, called her during office hours one day: "Do you know anything about computers?"

"I'm just sitting in front of one to bring our listings up to date."

"Drop everything and come to see me!"

The clerical uncle had heard that the State of Vatican City was looking to hire computer-literate young people. This was the early nineties; Annamaria quickly joined the Holy See's personnel.

Ten years later Annamaria is still living with her mother in their apartment in the Nomentana district in northeastern

Rome. "A thirty-five minute commute to and from the office," she says with a sigh. Romans like to work near where they live. In her mid-thirties now, she mentions without any prodding and with little conviction that she might get married "some day" but would continue working.

"It's a good job," she says. "Except for the crucifixes on the walls and the greenery and the flowers of the Vatican Gardens just around the corner, you might think you were in a bank. An efficient bank at that since the American cardinal has taken over." She is referring to Cardinal Edmund Casimir Szoka, the Polish-descended former archbishop of Detroit whom Pope John Paul II tapped to head the administrative arm of the pontifical state. Cardinal Szoka had a reputation as a crack manager in Detroit; he merged parishes to save money, despite protests from the congregations. In the Vatican he sought to bring some order to the jumble of papal finances.

Talking about work, Annamaria reports that many of her colleagues at the office are laymen, accountants like herself, some with college degrees. "It's numbers, numbers all day. We collect rents, pay salaries, audit expense statements, administer properties. Every now and then we run into matters that concern some special branch of the Holy See, but it's clear that the American cardinal wants to control all papal money affairs." Annamaria has seen Cardinal Szoka only a few times and has never spoken to him. Her immediate boss is a lawyer.

"How is the atmosphere at work? Cool, I should say. We do our jobs, there is little small talk, and everybody seems glad when we can go home. I surely am."

Does she have anything to do with the Vatican bank? "You mean the IOR?" Annamaria says, using the Italian acronym for the Institute for the Works of Religion, the Vatican banking agency. It had been in bad trouble during the 1980s. "Nothing at all. I know where they have their offices, close to the Gate of St. Anne where I get in every morning, but I have never been inside the IOR. They don't manage Vatican money, but deposits from religious orders and other clients. Not our business. Maybe the American cardinal knows what they are doing."

Annamaria says she goes to church with her mother in their neighborhood every Sunday but doesn't seem to be deeply interested in religion. She buys household supplies at the Annona, sometimes also for neighbors and friends. She doesn't appear to know many Vatican people outside her own office. The priestly uncle who got her the job has died, and her mother is ailing. "I rarely go out at night," she remarks. "Maybe to a movie once in a while. Mostly Mama and I watch TV in the evening and go to bed early."

Sister Matilda seems glad to be able to sound off after I have promised I wouldn't identify her, the order to which she belongs, or her curial job. I was introduced to her by another nun whom I have known for several years, and we meet in an empty waiting room at a church-affiliated private clinic where Sister Matilda receives ambulatory treatment.

The nun, in the simple garb of her congregation—recently modernized, she explains—is lively and articulate, apparently in her early fifties. She chuckles a lot and underlines her points with vigorous gestures.

She tells me that a great-great-uncle of hers once had been a bishop in one of the dioceses near Venice and that a cousin of hers is a monsignor. One of four children of a notary public and of a former schoolteacher, she studied foreign languages and philosophy in her hometown in the Veneto region and at the Catholic University of Milan, wanting to become a teacher like her mother.

In Milan her decision to enter the religious life "matured," Sister Matilda says without elaborating. Soon after graduation she started her novitiate in a community of hundreds of nuns in various places in northern Italy, Switzerland, Rome, and elsewhere. After a couple of years she was asked by her superiors to teach philosophy in a church-supported high school, first as a substitute, then full-time.

"Nearly twenty years a 'prof,' as the kids called me," Sister Matilda recalls, her dark eyes sparkling. "How fast those years went by! I really enjoyed the daily contact with young people nine or ten months every year; during vacations I was always looking forward to school starting again. I think there was real give-and-take in my classes, and the students—girls and boys—respected me. [One of her chuckles.] They surely made life hard for some of my lay colleagues and even for the religion teacher, a young, timid priest, but rarely for me."

Five years ago, the nun continues, out of the blue her mother superior informed her that she had been recommended for a position in the Vatican. " 'Who, me?' I asked incredulously," Sister Matilda recalls. "To this day I really don't know how they singled me out. It's true, all of those years I attended summer courses and evening classes in religious disciplines—scriptural exegesis, Saint Thomas Aquinas, canon law, you name it. Could one of the theologians who conducted those classes have mentioned my name? Or was it all a deal between mothers superior? I've never been able to find out. So much is being done in secrecy in the church."

Sister Matilda was sorry to give up teaching but was thrilled by the prospect of being employed "at the center of the universal church." She transferred to the Roman house of her congregation, where the nuns seemed puzzled by her reassignment. For the past five years Sister Matilda has been commuting six days a week between her convent and an office of the Curia.

Right now, she says, the job consists mainly of preparing drafts and occasional translations of documents that will be reviewed and eventually signed by one of her superiors, often an archbishop, sometimes a cardinal.

"I had more fun as a 'prof,' even though some kids tried to tease me," the nun says ruefully. "I didn't expect to land in a rigid bureaucracy. I might as well have ended up in the statistical department of the government, crunching numbers all day."

One of the things that most frustrates her, the nun points out, is that the "priests and prelates in the Curia treat us women, religious and lay, like children. I didn't know what male clerical arrogance and repression of women into infantilism were before I came to the Vatican. Look, the Code of Canon Law says somewhere that all Christians have equal dignity, which evidently also means women. We are actually second-class citizens at the Holy See."

Later I looked up in the church's lawbook what the nun had referred to. Canon 208 reads: "In virtue of their rebirth in Christ there exists among all the Christian faithful a true equality with regard to dignity and the activity whereby they all cooperate in the building up of the Body of Christ."

Sister Matilda is convinced she knows more about theology and liturgy than does her immediate boss, a monsignor who is getting on in years and is becoming nervous about not yet having made bishop. "He never discusses matters of faith with me, but from occasional remarks and what I hear him say on the phone, I know he really doesn't care a lot about religion. Bureaucratic procedure is everything for him—'How did we handle such cases in the past, Sister? Look up the precedents, please.' I am not sure he reads his breviary every day, and if he does, he may fall asleep over it."

Sister Matilda describes the atmosphere in her office as "full of hypocrisy" and clerical cant. "My boss often sighs to me in off moments, and I have overheard him saying to other people how sorry he is that he has no chance for hands-on pastoral work, for administering the sacraments, and for advising and helping persons in trouble. Why doesn't he volunteer to help out in some parish on the Roman outskirts the way some other priests who have special assignments do? Rome with all its ecclesiastics doesn't have enough parish clergy, strange though it sounds. The Vicariat imports priests from Poland and Latin America to staff all the parishes. The truth is that my monsignor entered the Vatican administration a few years after he was ordained and hasn't budged since then. From his housekeeper I know that on Sundays he sits at home, five minutes from the office, listens to music, and navigates the Internet."

Would she herself like to be a priest? I ask the nun. She blushes a little. "Frankly, I could handle it right now," she replies after a moment. "I know the prayers of the mass by heart and could do the other stuff. I am convinced, and so are quite a few of my fellow sisters, that nuns will be allowed at some future time to hear confessions, especially from women, and to perform what's required for the other sacraments. We don't say that aloud, at least not in the Vatican, but we hear and read what our fellow sisters in America, Germany, and other countries say. Female priesthood in the Catholic Church is bound to come."

Does Sister Matilda and her fellow sisters at the convent often talk about such aspirations? "You bet! And I also know that many nuns in the Curia feel the way I do, although we never say so to the clerics."

Vatican prelates don't like to discuss theology with women at all, says Helen, an American intern in one of the offices of the

New Curia. In Rome everybody calls her Elena, and she has many friends among the nuns, seminarians, and young priests in town who don't mind speaking about Saint Thomas Aquinas or Teilhard de Chardin with her. "Theology to me is an intellectual challenge," she explains.

Helen has attended Harvard Divinity School and traveled to Tübingen, Germany, to talk with Hans Küng, the Swiss priest-professor who questions papal infallibility. Through a Rome-trained bishop friend of her wealthy East Coast family, Helen has been able to put in a spell of work at the Vatican "to soak up the atmosphere and gather experience." She now sorts her office's English-language mail, which arrives in conspicuous volume, and revises translations done by others. She no longer tries to engage her clerical colleagues and superiors in weighty religious talk. Initial attempts to do so were discouraged. "I was given to understand to leave theology to the professionals."

Later, she muses, she may go into teaching or become a writer on religious matters. Would she consider entering an order of nuns? "Heavens, no," she snorts. "I'm not postulant material. Besides, few of the sisters I know in the Curia seem very happy."

Helen has quickly become fairly fluent in Italian and insists that a good knowledge of the language is essential in the Vatican. "It's still an Italianate outfit," she explains. "Despite the so-called internationalization of the Curia and the Polish pope, Italian remains the lingua franca here. Don't be misled by the encyclicals and all the other documents in Latin. The Synod Hall, where the bishops and the cardinals hold their work meetings, has installations for simultaneous translations because many of Their Excellencies and Their Eminences are unable to understand spoken Latin or take part in a debate in Latin. It's a far cry from the times of Leo X [Giovanni de'

Medici, 1513–21], who used to improvise witty hexameters, joking in Latin with the humanists of that age."

Not only was Helen struck by the Italianate atmosphere in the Vatican, she was even more surprised by the readiness, even eagerness, of non-Italian ecclesiastics to adjust to it. "Most of them become super-Roman," she scoffs. "They eat pasta every day and are siesta addicts."

Helen is also astonished that the Italian media devote so much space to Vatican affairs. "You'd think the pope is the king of Italy, and everything he says and does—and that's a lot—requires fullest coverage by the newspapers and television." She is, furthermore, scandalized by *L'Osservatore Romano*, which, she finds, "all the time meddles in Italian politics, and nobody here seems to find it inappropriate that the Vatican newspaper puts its nose into Italian affairs that absolutely aren't its business."

The Curia intern instead is a fan of *Famiglia Cristiana* (Christian Family), a weekly published by the Society of St. Paul, an Italian order known also as the Paolini Fathers. It's sold mainly in churches and is the Italian magazine with the largest circulation. "It's lively, broad-minded, and modern," Helen says. "It discusses topics like divorce or masturbation, and I find something interesting in each issue."

Roberta, who is thirty-four years old and has a university degree, works in an office of the Vatican Museums—and is proud of it. "It's a world-class institution," she says, "and I can see masterpieces by Michelangelo, Raphael, and other immortals whenever I want. By now I know every brush stroke of our treasures." The Sistine Chapel and the Borgia Apartment, frescoed by Pinturicchio, are part of the museum circuit, as are the Loggia and Stanze of Raphael.

"The crowds!" Roberta says with a sigh. "On some days, especially on one Monday each month when admission is free, twenty thousand people throng our galleries and corridors, and there are mob scenes when travel groups try to squeeze into the Sistine Chapel, which is already full as an egg."

Just before the start of the 2000 Jubilee, the Vatican opened a monumental new entrance to its museums. "I have heard that to build it cost more than forty billion lire [about $20 million], but we do produce a lot of money through entrance fees, and they don't spend so much on salaries for us." On inquiry later, I learned that the museum project included not only the new entrance but also consolidation of the foundations under a vast built-over area by ramming scores of concrete pillars into the subsoil. The former entrance to the museums, with its famous double-helix staircases built in 1932, is now for exiting only.

I ask Roberta how she got her job. When she mumbles something about a recommendation by "friends," I ask her on a hunch, "Are you with Opus Dei?"

She replies: "I live at home with my family—Opus Dei members stay together in residences." This doesn't really answer my question, because there are various classes of the organization's membership; far from all of its eighty thousand lay members live in Opus Dei houses. But I let it go at that and don't press the point.

Roberta tells me that plainclothes men of the Vatican security service mingle with the hordes of visitors all the time. "We are forever afraid that some crazy type will damage a priceless painting or sculpture, the way that nutcase attacked Michelangelo's *Pietà* in St. Peter's with a hammer [in 1972]." After visiting hours, Roberta says, security people thoroughly search the vast premises to make sure no outsider is hiding in some corner, intent on mischief during the night. An electronic alarm system is in operation around the clock.

The Vatican Museums include the Gallery of Modern Religious Art, opened in some thirty, mostly small, rooms in 1973—a pet project of Pope Paul VI, who collected late-nineteenth-century and twentieth-century paintings, graphics, and sculpture. Roberta doesn't think much of most of them. "There are a few fine works by Klee, Matisse, Chagall, and Kandinsky," she tells me, "but most of the stuff is just so-so, donated to Pope Paul, and arranged in a helter-skelter way. Our strength isn't in modern art but in the Italian Renaissance, when the popes gave commissions to magnificent artists."

Apart from the crush of visitors, how is the work climate in the museums? I ask. Roberta moans. "There are relatively few priests on our staff; some of the lay employees are intellectuals or think they are intellectuals, jealous like monkeys, jealous of anybody who talks to visiting scholars or experts, that sort of thing." Not unlike the work atmosphere in other cultural institutions elsewhere, I suggest.

Roberta likes to talk to knowledgeable visitors when she gets the chance. She wouldn't mind being hired someday by an art gallery or museum abroad, "and not only for the money but also for the experience."

Virginia, in her fifties, is the wife of an employee of Vatican City's technical services; they have been living in the same four-room apartment near the power station in the northeastern salient of the papal enclave's walls for many years. Now she is afraid that the pontifical real estate administration may shunt them to smaller quarters because their son has left for a job in Milan and their daughter will soon move out to get married.

Meeting Virginia in the home of her sister in Rome's Flaminio section, I ask her whether she knew Emanuela Orlandi, the Vatican teenager who vanished in 1983. "Did we know her? Where we live everybody knows everybody, it's like a small village. Two days before the girl disappeared, I saw her. I was taking our boy to the doctor because of a rash that turned out to be an allergy, and we passed her as she was walking to the Gate of St. Anne to get out. As always, she greeted me with a smile; she seemed in a pleasant mood. I told the security service about it later when they questioned all of us if we had any idea of what may have happened to Emanuela."

Virginia is convinced that the Vatican security people know more about Emanuela than they have let on. "They know everything," she suggests darkly. "They know also what we'll have for dinner at home tonight, although [chuckle] I don't know yet myself, leftovers probably. The security knows what's in my refrigerator and what I buy at the Annona, what we say on the phone, and what we watch on TV. When our boy was a student, he sometimes slept here on the sofa at my sister's so that the security people wouldn't know that he stayed out late."

Despite such surveillance, it is still a great privilege to reside in the Vatican, Virginia concedes. "We never see the Holy Father except on television and almost never go to St. Peter's Square. We go for Sunday mass at St. Anne's," the little parish church of Vatican City adjacent to the gate named after the same saint, opposite the Swiss Guards barracks.

"Ah, the Swiss!" Virginia exclaims with another chuckle. "My husband and I, we both are from the Abruzzi Mountains, so we understand mountain folk. Not everybody in the Vatican likes them, but we do. They are nice lads, all of them. Of course, they are a bit too fond of our wine, but there's nothing wrong with that."

. . .

Sister Emilia, daughter of a French mother and an Italian father, waited on tables in restaurants and cafeterias during vacations in her student years, which is why, she thinks, "Mother Superior, who knows almost everything about me," gives her those assignments. The occasional jobs, welcome interruptions to her convent life in Rome, include helping out at Domus Sanctae Marthae, the Vatican guest house.

"They wouldn't let me serve the Holy Father when he was the host at a luncheon for the entire College of Cardinals," she says regretfully. "I should have so much loved to do it. But I have come to know plenty of cardinals and archbishops. Whenever there is a buffet lunch, I have to help old prelates who have trouble moving to get the food they want."

One or another high prelate has asked her whether she'd like to take over the care of his private household, she reports, "but I wouldn't want to become some kind of live-in maid." Her stock reply to such offers is "Ask Mother Superior." She is pretty sure the head of her congregation won't let her go.

"At table those prelates become quite human," Sister Emilia says. "You wouldn't believe how they change from when you see them in church or in a procession—serious, the hands folded, looking neither left nor right. At lunch or dinner many of them like to joke with one another or with the service staff. They tell funny stories and talk from one table to another. And they all like their food, that's for sure. Everyone seems to love pasta, and they all drink wine, too, although a French archbishop whispered to me it's not so good—the Vatican might get hold of some better vintages; quite a few French wineries would be happy to donate a lot of bottles if they could advertise that they are suppliers to the Holy See."

• • •

Sister Veronica had for several years served as an assistant to the superior general of her large order before she was called to the Vatican to fill a vacant job in an important Curia department. She is now in her early fifties, stout but lively and, she says, quite happy with what she does. She won't discuss the nature of her duties in the Curia, because "I am sworn to silence."

She will speak, however, and volubly, about religious life in Rome: she doesn't think much of it. Sister Veronica comes from a family with roots in northern Italy and Switzerland that has produced at least one Swiss Guardsman for the pope and two priests during the last two generations. "We take our faith seriously," she remarks, giving to understand that the Romans don't.

"We are getting reports about flourishing Catholic life in Latin American countries and in Africa south of the Sahara all the time," Sister Veronica says. "I can disclose at least that much about the work in my department. That's heartening. I wish I could say the same about what I have seen and am seeing here."

Sister Veronica was already working in the Curia when she volunteered to take part, on her free weekends, in the "urban mission" campaign that the church conducted just in the city of the pontiffs, between 1996 and 1999. Proclaimed by Pope John Paul II in his capacity as bishop of Rome, and organized by the vicar of the diocese, Cardinal Camillo Ruini, the broad Catholic revival drive involved thousands of activists.

"A few monsignors and priests of the Curia also found time to participate," Sister Veronica reports. "There were many ecclesiastics and nuns from diverse institutions here, and plenty of lay volunteers. Funny, not all pastors in the Roman parishes were enthusiastic about the urban mission. They dutifully spoke about it from the pulpit but didn't do all that much to help

us. We went from house to house like the propagandists of the
new sects, distributed copies of the Gospel according to St.
Mark and of the Acts of the Apostles, spoke to people about
their problems, and urged them to go to church with their
children. In condominiums we tried to find families who would
hold weekly gospel readings and invite other people in the
same building to attend. And we impressed on them all the
importance of a religious education for their kids."

The urban mission initiative by the pope and his vicar was
apparently touched off by the realization that some Christian
denominations, such as the Jehovah's Witnesses and Pentecos-
tals, were advancing in Rome, and in particular had won many
new followers among the poor immigrants to the city. The
house-to-house canvassing by the Catholic evangelists as well
as the distributions of free Bible tracts copied the methods of
the rival proselytizers.

"The truth is that the vast majority of the Romans still
think of themselves as Catholics but don't really care either for
us or for the sects. They care for soccer, television, a new car,
a trip to the seaside, and good food. Religion for most families
ends with First Communion of their kids—they don't even
want the sacrament of confirmation for them. Young people
are interested in rock music, motor scooters and motorcycles,
the pub, the discotheque, yelling until they are hoarse in the
Olympic Stadium to support Roma or Lazio [soccer teams], sex,
and maybe drugs."

Reminded that the pope nevertheless draws big crowds at
every one of his frequent public appearances, Sister Veronica
says, "They are mostly tourists and out-of-towners. Of course,
the Romans have always enjoyed a good show. But what we
have here is an essentially post-Christian society. Observe how
quickly some priests race through the liturgy when they say
mass: it seems that even a part of the diocesan clergy is bored

with the ritual. Our sharpest theologians speak of a 'silent apostasy' of Catholics in Rome."

The austere nun of the Curia also voices what sounds like faint criticism of Pope John Paul II himself: "On the one hand, we insist that abortion is always a grave sin and that the Roman Catholic Church is the only true church of Jesus—unpopular truths today. On the other hand, the Holy Father goes to synagogues and mosques and apologizes to the Eastern Orthodox, Protestants, Jews, and Muslims for what Catholics did to them. All very edifying, but won't a lot of our people be led to believe that all faiths have really the same value? I have lately heard a term for this kind of attitude in the Vatican: creeping syncretism—the notion that there is no serious difference between what people believe as long as they believe in God."

Number Rosalba Nicoletti among the Vatican's women. The white-haired widow has no church job nor does she live in the papal state, but you can see her almost every afternoon praying in front of the glass coffin that contains the embalmed body of Pope John XXIII in St. Peter's.

"I'm glad they brought good Papa Giovanni [Pope John] up here," Signora Nicoletti says. "That saves me the narrow stairs down to the grottoes." Following Pope John's death in 1963, after only four years and seven months on the papal throne, he was laid to rest in a tomb in the grottoes below St. Peter's, where many other pontiffs are buried, too. When a recent check showed that his remains were surprisingly well preserved, Pope John Paul II ordered them to be transferred to the basilica above the grottoes.

"I visited Papa Giovanni also when he was down there and one could see only the stone coffin and the flowers that people like me brought him," Signora Nicoletti reminisces. "Some of the regulars nod at me and I nod back, but we don't talk; it's a holy place. The guards all know me and I know them, and I know some of the pickpockets, too. Sometimes I whisper to tourists to be careful. Foreigners often carry their wallets in the back pockets of their pants as if to invite thieves to help themselves."

Signora Nicoletti doesn't care, maybe doesn't even know, that the altar to the left of the pontifical altar at the center is dedicated to Saint Jerome. She probably doesn't know either that Saint Jerome was an early-Christian scholar who translated the Bible from Hebrew into Latin (the Vulgate). To her it's not the altar of Saint Jerome but the altar of Papa Giovanni.

"All popes are good men," she says loyally, "but Papa Giovanni was the best. He'll be a saint very soon; he works a lot of miracles. I started visiting him after my poor husband died. I prayed that he should go straight to heaven, and I pray for a good death for myself so that I meet Antonio [her late husband] again in heaven. I prayed to get a pension without any hitch, and I did. I pray to Papa Giovanni also when someone in the family or a neighbor is sick. And I prayed especially hard when my great-nephew who is a Carabinieri sergeant was sent to Bosnia; he has come back all right."

In a solemn beatification ceremony in September 2000, Pope John Paul II proclaimed his predecessor "blessed." In the same rite another predecessor, Pope Pius IX (1846–78), was also beatified, but he is much less popular among the faithful than is Pope John. The latter appears to be well on the way toward official sainthood; the examination of his remains that preceded and prompted their transfer to the altar of Saint Jerome was part of the prescribed procedure for eventual canonization. More miracles must be certified—usually remissions from sickness that according to physicians cannot be rationally explained.

Once every week Signora Nicoletti takes two buses to visit her husband's grave at the Flaminio Cemetery on the far northern outskirts of Rome. The other days she walks from her home for twenty minutes to St. Peter's and another twenty minutes back. "Only if the weather is very bad, I stay at home and pray in front of the big picture of Papa Giovanni in my bedroom."

She is sorry that she wasn't in St. Peter's Square when Pope John XXIII gave his first apostolic benediction to the Romans and to the world following his election in 1958. "I saw him only on TV; I was a kid, but we all felt, 'This is a good pope.'"

IX

WHAT THE WOMEN WANT

Step into any Catholic church in Rome or Rio de Janeiro, in Lagos or Manila or Dublin for Sunday mass or on a workday and you will in all likelihood see more women than men in the pews. The all-male clergy of Roman Catholicism has at all times had stronger support from women than from men. In addition to the many millions of laywomen loyal to the church, there is an army of nuns—more than 700,000, almost twice the number of priests. To some extent they have taken over ecclesiastic work from the churchmen; they also run schools, staff hospitals, and manage charities.

Yet the Vatican's convoluted bureaucracy doesn't include any one unit specifically addressing women's affairs, aspirations, and problems. Nor is there any woman official in the Roman Curia who can authoritatively advise the pope or speak to public opinion about the female condition. In 1974 Pope Paul VI set up a commission on the role of women in the church; from the outset it was made clear that the body would not be allowed to take up the possibility of ordaining women to the priesthood, and its work fizzled out eventually. Celibate men, mostly elderly, continue laying down the Vatican's laws for women.

The Curia's agency most closely concerned with issues of major interest to women is the Pontifical Council for the Family, established by Pope John Paul II in 1981. Its offices, together with other sections of the New Curia is in the Palace of St. Calixtus. The council is composed of nearly twenty husband-and-wife couples from various countries, under the leadership of a presidential committee of a dozen cardinals and as many lesser prelates. The permanent staff includes a few laywomen and is supplemented by a small crowd of consultants—bishops, priests, laymen and -women who show up in Rome from time to time or communicate with the council by mail or electronically.

The council's main concern is "responsible procreation," meaning the fight against any form of birth control that isn't complete abstinence from intercourse or the so-called rhythm method of abstinence limited to the period of ovulation. Other stated fields of the agency's research and activities are sex education; biogenetics, including artificial insemination; homosexuality; AIDS; pornography; prostitution; and drug abuse. The council publishes a magazine, *Family and Life*, three times a year and issues instructions and advice to bishops everywhere.

To Pope John Paul II the fight against birth control by artificial means and against abortion has been a main concern (critics say, a fixation). He created a Pontifical Academy for Life in 1994. It consists of seventy scientists named by the pope, a few women among them, who pledge to uphold the church's teachings on bioethics. The group has permanent offices near the Vatican and holds plenary meetings once in a while, run by the academy's vice president and chief spokesman, an Italian bishop. The academy's president is the head of the Catholic University of Santiago, Chile, a layman. The chief purpose of this body appears to be to give academic prestige and credibility to the papacy's positions on issues involving human biology.

Among the half a dozen nuns and laywomen whom John Paul II appointed to the Pontifical Academy for Life was an old friend of his, Wanda Póltawska of the Pontifical Academy of Theology in Kraków. Professor Póltawska (with her husband, Andrzej) also served as a consultant to the Pontifical Council for the Family. Pope John Paul II was known to also greatly value her advice regarding the church and its hierarchy in Poland.

Catholic women might expect consideration from another section of the New Curia, the Pontifical Council for Justice and Peace. Its field includes human rights—which surely also comprise the rights of women. Yet those are passed over in silence by the official Vatican description (in *Annuario Pontificio*) of what the council is supposed to do. According to this text, it gathers "information on violations of human rights," especially the right to religious freedom, besides striving for social justice and world peace.

The Pontifical Council for Justice and Peace, set up by Pope Paul VI in 1976, numbers a few laywomen and nuns among its members, permanent staff, and consultants. Its seat is in the Palace of St. Calixtus. This curial body advises the pope's Secretariat of State and the pontiff himself on the problems with which it deals, but there is no sign that women's predicaments are conspicuously among them.

The church's two thousand or so organizations of nuns are monitored, along with religious orders of men, by a branch of the Curia that was long known as the Congregation of the Religious. To accommodate new types of religious associations, it has recently been clumsily renamed the Congregation for Institutes of Consecrated Life and Societies of Apostolic Life.

The congregation, housed in one of the buildings just outside St. Peter's Square, operates with a relatively small staff of officials, including a few nuns, and scores of consultants. Much work is done on a lower level by national, regional, and international unions of the superiors of male and female religious orders.

Much of this department's business has to do with problems within religious organizations, especially disputes between them and local bishops or civil authorities. Lately there has also been a rising number of petitions from monks, friars, and nuns who seek release from their vows. At the same time, in several European countries and in North America the number of novices for men's orders and nunneries has been sharply declining. Many religious orders are shrinking and want to sell or reconvert convents they no longer need. Conversely, Mother Teresa's Missionaries of Charity has no dearth of postulants from many nations, despite (or because of) the austerity of their rule.

A perturbing problem the Congregation of the Religious and other Vatican departments have had to grapple with lately is alleged sexual exploitation of nuns by priests. Complaints about such occurrences had reached Rome for some time, including a circumstantiated report by the mother superior of the White Sisters (Missionary Sisters of Our Lady of Africa), an order with twelve hundred members and headquarters in Rome.

The matter was brought into the open by the *National Catholic Reporter* of Kansas City, Missouri. Questioned about the affair in March 2001, the Vatican spokesman, Dr. Navarro-Valls, stated that "the problem is known and is restricted to one geographical area [Africa]. The issue is being dealt with in collaboration with the bishops." Some negative situations, the spokesman added, must not obscure the "often heroic attitude of the overwhelming majority of monks, nuns, and priests."

From the published reports, it would appear that priests and seminarians getting sexual favors from religious sisters isn't an exclusively African phenomenon. The *National Catholic Reporter* presented signed statements from religious sisters in twenty-three countries charging that priests and missionaries had induced them into sex. In some cases the seducer urged the woman to take the Pill or undergo an abortion, the nuns alleged. It seems that young nuns sent to Rome for study have had similar experiences. Female religious are trained to regard priests as something like higher beings and often find it difficult to resist advances by them.

Catholic Feminism

The Vatican has been aware since the middle of the twentieth century of growing vexation among educated Catholic women at being marginalized by their church. Something like a women's liberation movement was gaining strength among female churchgoers and even nuns, the Curia realized. Ripples of Catholic feminism had already reached the Holy See by the time of the Second Vatican Council, called by Pope John XXIII in 1962, to the dismay of Curia conservatives, to bring about an *aggiornamento* (updating) of the church.

A number of women "auditors" were asked to follow the work of the council fathers but were not allowed to address the assembly of more than two thousand bishops from all over the world in St. Peter's. Vatican II enacted important reforms such as the introduction of local languages (the "vernacular") instead of Latin in the celebration of mass.

The council considered the status of women in the church only in passing and left things essentially unchanged. The council fathers reconfirmed the male monopoly of the priesthood, the rule of priestly celibacy, and the ban on abortion. When the issue of artificial birth control (the Pill) came up, Pope Paul VI—who had meanwhile succeeded John XXIII— stepped in to announce that he would in due course make a personal decision on the basis of advice from a scientific commission that had been set up in 1962. By 1967, a year and a half after Vatican II had concluded, the commission in a majority report advocated a change in the church's stand: it should be up to the individual married couple to make a conscientious decision as to whether to practice birth control.

After long agonizing, Pope Paul VI yielded to a powerful group of conservatives in the Curia and set aside the advice from the scientific commission. In his 1968 encyclical *Humanae Vitae* (Of Human Life) he reaffirmed the church's rigid *no* regarding any form of artificial birth control. The encyclical set off an ecclesiastical and media fire storm such as the Vatican had not experienced since Pope Pius IX in 1870 pressured the First Vatican Council into voting the dogma of papal infallibility. Liberal critics of Paul VI within the church, including many women, showed bitterness and dismay; blistering attacks came from non-Catholic sources in many parts of the world.

By now the Curia knows through confidential reports from bishops as well as from public-opinion polls and the international press that the papacy's strictures concerning birth control are widely ignored by the Catholic rank and file. "Supermarket Catholicism" or "cafeteria Catholicism" is demonstrably gaining ground among the faithful, particularly in the industrialized nations: laypeople pick and choose instead of buying the whole package, heeding some papal teachings while disregarding others.

A part of the lower clergy is known to silently condone such selective faith. Some of the bishops turn a blind eye in practice, although they officially profess strict adherence to the Vatican line and assure Rome of their loyalty. Since there may always be some conservative zealot denouncing liberals to the Curia, considerable episcopal finesse is required.

A private poll of hundreds of thousands of young women and men who enthusiastically attended an international Catholic youth rally in Rome in August 2000, marking one of the high points of the church's Jubilee Year, found that a majority of them thought that premarital sex was not a grave sin, much less so than were intolerance, racism, or environmental misdeeds. Sanitation department workers told reporters that "many" condoms had been found on the grounds of Rome II State University on the far southeastern outskirts of Rome after the young participants had held an all-night vigil before outdoor mass celebrated by Pope John Paul II in the morning. The pontiff was joyously greeted by the crowd.

Rome knows that many well-schooled women, especially among the nuns, consider it outrageous that the priesthood is closed to them. An even larger segment of the church's rank and file, women and men, is apparently convinced that the time has come to permit priests to marry. The Vatican's reaction so far has been to stonewall, although over the past few decades thousands of priests have abandoned their ministry to get married with or without curial dispensation.

Liberal churchmen in Rome who will never allow themselves to be identified for fear of Vatican reprisals admit in confidential conversations that, rather sooner than later, the scarcity of priests will force the papacy to drop the rule of clerical celibacy and eventually also to admit female priests.

Such reforms may "well come for the wrong reasons," argues Garry Wills, a Catholic layman and distinguished historian, "because of panic at the perception that the priesthood is becoming increasingly gay."*

Complaints about offenses by homosexual priests or even bishops had reached the Vatican in growing numbers for some time. In 1995 the archbishop of Vienna, Cardinal Hans Hermann Groër, resigned and went to live in a convent amid allegations that in earlier years he had sexually molested students for the priesthood. Since then, sex offenses by gay clergymen have been reported from various countries including Pope John Paul II's own homeland, Poland. In one such affair the archbishop of Poznan, Juliusz Paetz, a friend of John Paul II, had to resign in March 2002.

The Roman Curia apparently realized it was confronted with a very serious problem only in early 2002, when U.S. media spotlighted the sentencing of a priest from the Boston archdiocese to nine to ten years in prison for indecent assault on a ten-year-old boy. The defendant, it was learned, had long been targeted by rumors as a child molester. At this point the Boston archdiocese turned over to Massachusetts state authorities the names of at least eighty priests who in the previous several years had been accused of abusing children or teenagers.

Similar cases of clerical pedophilia or sex offenses against adolescent boys in various other dioceses of the United States have come to public attention. The Roman Catholic Church paid out hundreds of millions of dollars to victims of alleged sexual crimes by priests in out-of-court settlements of civil lawsuits that were based on claims that the minors had suffered lasting psychological damage. Many of the payments seem to have been made on the condition that the plaintiffs keep silent. (Such gag orders are a frequent feature of private settlements.)

---

*Garry Wills, *Papal Sin: Structures of Deceit* (New York: Doubleday, 2000), p. 195.

The Boston criminal trial and the other disclosures about pedophile priests have caused a media outcry in the United States. Requests for comment by the Vatican remained fruitless for some weeks, until John Paul II personally spoke out. In his customary Maundy Thursday message to all the priests and bishops of his church, the pope dealt with the issue of sex offenses by homosexual members of the clergy in seventeen lines, without mentioning specifically what they had done.

John Paul II declared himself deeply shocked "by the sins of some of our brethren who have betrayed the [divine] grace received by their ordination" to the priesthood. The pontiff lamented that the "grave scandals" were casting "dark shadows of suspicion" over all the other priests who were carrying out their ministry honestly and sometimes "with heroic charity." The pope expressed the church's "solicitude" for the victims of sinning priests and said it would "respond according to truth and justice to each painful situation," mindful of human frailty and trusting in the healing power of divine grace.

Such pontifical phraseology failed to lessen media outrage and allay the dismay of many Roman Catholics in the United States.

In April 2002 Pope John Paul II summoned the U.S. cardinals to Rome to discuss with them the widening scandal. Eight American cardinals and eight cardinals of the Curia took part in the confidential debates, attended in part by the pontiff, April 23 and 24.

In a published address to the heads of the hierarchy—the cardinals—in the United States John Paul II said that the guilty members of the clergy had committed acts that were a "tremendous sin in the eyes of God and a crime toward civil society."

The pope blamed the American church for not having realized sooner the gravity of the problem. The two-day Vatican meeting ended with a joint declaration by the U.S. cardinals deploring that the American episcopacy had been unable to protect the church from scandal; calling for a day of prayer and penitence by the entire Catholic Church in the United States; and instituting a special procedure for expelling guilty members of the clergy from the priesthood.

Participants in the Vatican session said that the issues of priestly celibacy and the admission of women to holy orders had not been brought up at any point of the discussions.

Hard-line Roman theologians explain that the exclusion of women from the priestly office is unchangeable divine law, whereas the rule of celibacy for clerics is church law and may be abrogated—although that isn't likely to happen.

One of the many clerical jokes that always make the rounds of seminaries and church colleges has a bishop whispering during a boring synod meeting: "Whatever they say, ecclesiastics will eventually be allowed to marry, and there will be woman priests, too." "Ah, my friend," the other bishop whispers back, "we won't see it. Our children and grandchildren will."

Try to discuss Roman Catholic feminism with a prelate of the Curia and you will probably get a brush-off. "An American deviation," you may be told, "an offshoot from women's lib." Actually, disaffection of Roman Catholic women because of the Vatican's inflexible conservatism is also strong in Europe and has publicly been voiced in the Netherlands, Belgium, Germany, Switzerland, and Austria. It is felt also in Rome and throughout Italy.

A nursing sister in her forties in a Roman clinic confided: "A copy of the Heinemann book has been going from hand to hand, from cell to cell in our house like subversive or indecent literature." She was referring to *Eunuchs for the Kingdom of Heaven* by Uta Ranke-Heinemann, which came out in Italian translation in 1990 soon after its publication in Germany.*

The author, a daughter of a former president of West Germany, Gustav Heinemann, converted to Roman Catholicism in 1953. She was a professor of Catholic theology at the University of Essen but was dismissed from that position by the church authorities after she questioned the dogma of Jesus' virgin birth. She remained a member of the university's state-appointed faculty as professor of history of religion. In her book, based on copious research, Ranke-Heinemann cites many sources, from the Fathers of the Church to modern popes, to prove that "hatred of women" by male celibates is diffuse within the church of Rome.

First Lady of the Vatican

John Paul I, whom the Romans quickly and affectionaly dubbed "the smiling pope," reigned for only thirty-three days, but he did a few remarkable things: he was the first pontiff in history to assume a double name to honor both of his two predecessors, John XXIII and Paul VI; he did away with the tiara, the pontifical triple crown symbolizing the popes' archaic claim to have been set by God above emperors and kings; and he baffled theologians by hinting at a female element of divinity.

On September 10, 1978, two weeks after his election to the papacy, John Paul I in a brief address to a crowd of the faithful in St. Peter's Square said from the open window of his study: "God isn't just our father; God is also our mother." He

---

*Published also in English: Uta Ranke-Heinemann, translated by Peter Heinegg, *Eunuchs for the Kingdom of Heaven: Women, Sexuality and the Catholic Church* (New York: Doubleday, 1990).

explained that whenever in sickness or misery we call for our mother, we really invoke the Creator.

The "smiling pope" surely wasn't improvising. He was widely read; he had written profiles of remarkable personages for a diocesan newspaper; and he was known to prepare carefully his sermons and speeches, even seemingly casual remarks. Had he lived longer, he might have elaborated on his concept of the Godhead having a feminine aspect.

Some Christian thinkers had been speculating on the problem before John Paul I. They occasionally suggested that the third person of the Trinity—the Holy Spirit—may be female, or male and female. Apparently, friends or aides of the "smiling pope" asked him after the September 10, 1978, address what he meant by God being also our mother. Oh, it's not an invention of mine, he was quoted as having replied; "it's all in Isaiah."

John Paul I was probably referring to Isaiah 66: 9–13: "Shall not I that make others to bring forth children myself bring forth, saith the Lord. . . . As one whom the mother caresseth so will I comfort you: and you shall be comforted in Jerusalem."

For the successor to John Paul I, the female principle in Christian faith was embodied in the Mother of God. The future Pope John Paul II had from his early years been an ardent devotee of the Virgin Mary. To him the Madonna in heaven may have been a sacred surrogate for his own mother, who died when he was a small boy and of whom he could have had only faint recollections. He appears to have always idealized virginity.

The cult of the Virgin Mary in Roman Catholicism has been criticized by Protestants as excessive, even idolatrous. The Second Vatican Council in 1964 in its dogmatic constitution on the church, *Lumen Gentium* (The Light of Humanity), strongly urged "theologians and preachers to refrain as much from all false exaggeration as from too summary an attitude in considering the special dignity of the Mother of God." In other words, neither go overboard in the cult of the Blessed Virgin nor downplay it.

As cardinal archbishop of Kraków, the future Pope John Paul II attended Vatican II and cannot have been unaware of the debates on Mariology within Roman Catholicism.

As the spiritual leader of an archdiocese with hundreds of thousands of rural and industrial worker families, Cardinal Wojtyla was also attentive to the female condition. He knew many women personally and—as old group photos show—used to make outings into the countryside with female friends and their children in a relaxed mood. The widely traveled and well-informed Polish prelate could not remain blind to Catholic feminist stirrings. For him to appease the impatient women in the church's rank and file, it clearly wasn't going to be enough to stress the cult of the Madonna.

The Virgin's "special dignity" had been enhanced in 1870 by the dogma of Immaculate Conception and in 1950 by the dogma of her bodily assumption to heaven. All-out Marianists were lobbying for acknowledging the Madonna as "co-redemptress," but Vatican II formally reaffirmed that there is only one Redeemer or mediator between humankind and God, Jesus.

In his address a little more than an hour after his election to the pontifical throne on October 16, 1978, John Paul II, speaking from the central loggia of St. Peter's, said: "I was afraid to receive this nomination [as head of the church] but I accepted it in the spirit of obedience to our Lord and in the total confidence in his mother, the Most Holy Madonna." Commentators at once pointed out that by paying such a tribute to the Virgin Mary in his very first public statement as pope, John

Paul II hadn't helped ecumenical efforts to reconcile Roman Catholics and Protestants.

The new pontiff chose a coat of arms featuring a golden cross and the letter M (for Mary) on a blue field; his lifelong motto: *Totus Tuus* (all yours), signifying total devotion to the Madonna.

Soon after moving into the pontifical living quarters on the top floor of the Apostolic Palace, John Paul II had an image of the "Black Madonna" of Czestochowa in Poland put up in his private chapel. Noting that St. Peter's Square with all its statuary lacked any visual reference to Our Lady, he had placed on a spur of the Apostolic Palace's west wing a picture of the Madonna that is visible from most points of the square.

John Paul II's sixth encyclical, *Redemptoris Mater* (The Redeemer's Mother), in 1987, was entirely devoted to the Virgin. In his many travels he made a point of visiting Marian shrines—Loreto (Italy), Guadalupe (Mexico), Lourdes (France), Maria Zell (Austria), Fátima (Portugal), and others; of course, he also made yet another pilgrimage to the Jasna Gora (Mountain of Light) monastery near Czestochowa to venerate its "Black Madonna."

On May 13, 2000, the nineteenth anniversary of the attempt on his life, Pope John Paul II returned to Fátima. On that date in 1917 three shepherd children in Fátima reported that a "white lady" had appeared and talked to them. John Paul II declared himself convinced that his life was saved by the Madonna, who had deflected the bullets fired by his Turkish assailant. During an outdoor ceremony attended by a huge crowd, Cardinal Angelo Sodano, the papal secretary of state, disclosed that the Madonna in one of her appearances had told the three shepherd children that at some future time an attack on a pope would be made. Thus the "third secret of Fátima" was at last revealed; two other supposed prophecies by the Virgin Mary, involving Russia, had been made known earlier.

Before Pope John Paul II left for Ukraine in June 2001, he said he placed his journey under the special protection of the Madonna, venerated in that country by both Catholic and Orthodox Christians.

It was during a visit to a Marian shrine, the National shrine of the Immaculate Conception in Washington, D.C., early in his pontificate that John Paul II was personally confronted by a moderate Catholic feminist. The president of the Leadership Conference of Women Religious, Sister Theresa Kane, wearing secular dress, read to him an appeal, asking in veiled terms for female access to the priesthood. The Polish pope said nothing, just lightly touched her hair.

By that time many American nuns had shed their traditional religious habits, and quite a few had abandoned the orders or congregations; thousands of others were to follow. Similar ferment among nuns was also occurring in various European nations.

In 1985, following consultations with Curia officials and theologians—but hardly with female advisers—John Paul II issued an apostolic letter (an authoritative papal document a little less solemn than an encyclical) on women. It is known by its first Latin words as *Mulieris Dignitatem* (Woman's Dignity). The text reaffirmed the church's bans on artificial birth control and abortion; the pope also gave to understand he considered virginity a higher state of female existence than marriage and motherhood.

John Paul II developed the themes of *Mulieris Dignitatem* in a *Letter to the Women of the World* just before the Fourth United Nations Conference on Women in Beijing in 1995. It is written in a peculiar blend of leaden curial language and flights of rhetoric in the characteristic style of a pontiff who has composed and published free-verse poetry. In the 1985 apostolic letter the pope had thanked "the Most Holy Trinity for the mystery of women." In 1995 he extended his gratitude to each and every woman, whether mother, spouse, daughter, sister, worker, or nun: "Thank you, woman, for the very fact that you are woman!"

John Paul II deplored antifemale discrimination, also by "not a few sons of the church," and hailed the "liberation of women from any form of coercion and domination." He noted that women all too often are valued more for their looks than for their brains and sensibility.

The papal letter strongly supported equal opportunities for women in education, professional life, and politics. It condemned sexual exploitation and violence that damages girls and women in a "diffuse hedonistic and mercantile culture." Abortion, the text declared, "remains always a grave sin."

Praising "the genius of women," the pope advocated more space for it in social life and in the church. But four paragraphs later he forcefully restated the Catholic Church's rejection of any female role in the ministry. Jesus by "free and sovereign decision," John Paul II argued, had reserved the office of pastor to men, as proved by the gospel and recognized by constant church tradition.

A Jesuit scholar, Thomas J. Reese, commented: "Whether an all-male hierarchy will be able to satisfy women with such a platform in the long run is unlikely." Father Reese, a senior fellow at the Woodstock Theological Center at Georgetown University, warned that the Vatican's attempts to silence the debate about possible ordination of women to the priesthood would increase female anger. "If the church loses educated women in the twenty-first century the way it lost European working-class males in the nineteenth century, it will be in serious trouble."*

Sister Matilda, who was quoted earlier in this book, suggested that in order to maintain the support of modern women, the church should at least revive the early-Christian office of deaconess right away. "The Second Vatican Council restored the male diaconate," the nun said. "It admitted married deacons and empowered them to administer baptism, bless marriages, read Scripture to congregations, and carry out other liturgical functions. Couldn't women, too, take part in the ministry in such ways? It would be a breakthrough, opening to them at least the lowest level of priesthood. More would come later."

In the time of the apostles, Sister Matilda pointed out, Christian communities were looked after also by deaconesses. "From the Letter of St. Paul to the Romans [16:1] we even know the name of one of them, Phoebe, 'who is in the ministry of the church,' in the apostle's words."

At the Vatican, the nun suggested, more women should be promoted to the upper ranks of the administration, and the Curia should get a new department or secretariat specializing in women's affairs. "It won't do to tell us all the time to take the Madonna as an example without really trying to solve our problems here on earth."

Pope John Paul II's 1995 *Letter to the Women of the World* concludes with a lyrical tribute to the Virgin Mary as the ideal woman: "The church sees in Mary the supreme expression of the 'female genius' and finds in her a source of unceasing inspiration." Our Lady in heaven thus is the First Lady of the papal government. The Vatican's flesh-and-blood women so far are mere handmaidens.

---

*Thomas J. Reese, *Inside the Vatican: The Politics and Organization of the Catholic Church* (Cambridge, Mass.: Harvard University Press, 1996), p. 276.

INDEX